Signs & Mysteries

Signs & Mysteries

Revealing Ancient Christian Symbols

℘

By MIKE AQUILINA

Illustrations by LEA MARIE RAVOTTI

Our Sunday Visitor Publishing Division
Our Sunday Visitor, Inc.
Huntington, Indiana 46750

For Teresa Carmella and Maria Crista

Our Sunday Visitor Publishing Division
Our Sunday Visitor, Inc.
200 Noll Plaza
Huntington, IN 46750

ISBN: 978-1-59276-450-1   (Inventory No. T687)

LCCN: 2008930870

Cover design by Lindsey Luken
Illustrations by Lea Marie Ravotti
Interior Design by Sherri L. Hoffman

PRINTED IN THE UNITED STATES OF AMERICA

Contents

ℱ

Introduction
Love in the Ruins

☙

It's not every day that an archeologist goes digging in the desert and discovers a new method of evangelization. But that's what happened to Dr. Emma Loosley of the University of Manchester, England, when she began her doctoral research in Syria in 1997. She went there to study the architecture of ancient Christian churches, now ruins in the hundreds of "ghost towns" that dot the barren hills between Antioch and Aleppo. She was most interested in their symbols and structures, the subtle relationship between form and function.

Setting up her residence in Aleppo, Dr. Loosley was surprised to find that the local Christians knew nothing about the history of the nearby ruins. Christians are a minority in Muslim-dominated Syria, and some have grown disenchanted with both the land and their religion. In school they learn little about the role of Christianity in ancient Syria — or the importance of Syria in the ancient Church. Thus, as Syrians, they feel alienated from Christianity; yet, as Christians, they feel alienated from their own country as well as the wider Church. Dr. Loosley observed that, in Aleppo, many old men opted to play backgammon outdoors on Sunday morning rather than attend the liturgy. Many young Christians simply left the country.

She suspected that their disenchantment had something to do with their historical disconnect. She wrote: "These men were alienated from the Church through ignorance and needed to be educated about their past." She decided to do something about it.

In 1997 she began taking groups of Christians from Aleppo to the Limestone Massif, to the west of the city, in order to examine the inscriptions and carvings they found there. She explained the symbols carved and scratched into walls in churches and homes. The Syrians in her groups ranged in age from late teens through senior citizens. Together, she discussed with them "how this kind of cultural awareness tied them more closely to the land than they had previously thought. In turn this caused them to question their self-imposed perception of themselves as 'outsiders' and to think in terms of a wider 'Syrian' identity."

She brought a deacon along, and the group prayed together in the ancient ruins.

And it worked. The older folks were fascinated to learn the meaning and antiquity of the symbols of their faith, and they went back to church. The women's Bible-study groups from the city parishes started organizing their own pilgrimages to the ghost towns. And Dr. Loosley found that young people who had taken her tours ended up as the citizens "least likely to emigrate." Such is the power of the faith "ever ancient, ever new" when the ancient symbols are proclaimed anew.

The lesson has universal applications. I believe that the same principles apply, by extension, to westerners who take up the study of the symbols of Christian antiquity. American Christians, after all, learn little of our religious history in the public schools; and we can, at times, feel somewhat alien in this land of abortion license. But Christians who truly

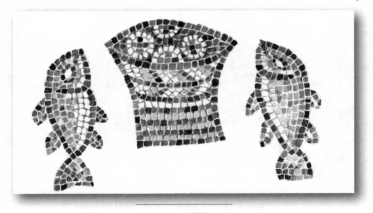

Loaves and fishes.
Mosaic from the Church of Multiplication. Galilee, Israel. Fifth century.
For more about fish symbolism, see Chapter 2 , The Fish.

know the cross, and the fish, and the lamb, and the lighting of the lamps — those who truly know the ancient symbols of the Church's doctrines and rites — are Christians who are rooted in the faith, and they know their roots run very deep indeed. They are less likely to leave the community, less likely to take interest in another religion, and less likely to choose backgammon over liturgy on a Sunday morning.

This is not a work of scholarship, but an act of devotion — an act of piety toward our ancestors, so that we might learn to see the world once again with their eyes, and to pray and live as they once prayed and lived.

Just after the turn of the second millennium, Pope Benedict XVI noted that "a highly technological age like our own . . . risks losing the ability to appreciate signs and symbols." He called upon Christian authors and teachers to present "the meaning of the signs contained in the rites." And so we have — I, the author, and Lea Marie Ravotti, the illustrator — in hope that you, in turn, will take up the task for your family, your parish, and your friends.

Chapter 1
The Background

❦

Ever since the creation of the world his invisible nature,
namely, his eternal power and deity, has been clearly
perceived in the things that have been made.
Romans 1:20

Several years ago, I was staying in Rome at an old hotel that was undergoing renovation. As the crew went about their work, they would fairly regularly turn up artifacts from various points in the city's long history — a glass bottle, a ceramic flask. And they'd line them up along the outside of the windowsill by the exit I used each morning. During the same trip, I visited a residence whose construction project, originally intended to be a garage, became a museum instead — a permanent exhibit of Jewish and Christian antiquities, identifiable by their distinctive marks: an anchor, a candelabra, a cross.

In that city, even at dusty work sites, my most remote Christian ancestors seemed near to me.

And so it is in all the lands where the Church first grew, where it emerged from the synagogues and the schools and the tenements. A friend of mine — an anthropologist who lived among the Coptic Christians in Egypt — summed it up for me in a memorable phrase: "In the desert, history is the thing that goes crunch under your feet."

Another friend, an American who lived with Arab Christians in Syria, tells me that shepherd boys — and sheep, too — often turn up lamps and other pottery that is identifiably Christian. The vessels bear the telltale signs: the fish, the dove, the sheaf of wheat, the palm branch.

Strange emblems from a long-ago time, these symbols still emerge unexpectedly from dark places, on objects large and small, in places public

Peacock and vine. Detail from the ivory throne of Archbishop Maximian of Ravenna,
A.D. 546–556 (now in Museo Archivescovile, Ravenna).
For more about peacock symbolism, see Chapter 9, The Peacock.

and private: in the casket of a forgotten nobleman, on the upper side of a ceramic lamp, on the bottom of a gilt-glass tumbler.

In the catacombs — the underground burial chambers of the early Christians — tourists encounter the symbols in variety and abundance. In several inscriptions, we see them arrayed like a coded message or a rebus puzzle: a dove, an anchor, a lamb, and then a man's name: Faustinianus.

These symbols are, in one sense, quite ordinary; they are commonplace items from everyday life in the ancient world. And so we might take them for granted, overlook them. But they're there for a reason. This is obvious by the care with which they were made, but also by the sheer repetition of each individual symbol. When we see these signs, how can we help sensing we have received an urgent message, telegraphic, cryptic, from a distant family member?

Many of these symbols were clearly not decorations. Some were hastily and crudely scratched into plaster. Others were carved, with painstaking effort and at great cost, into the sides of burial caskets. Yet, among the rich and poor, among those in persecution and those at peace, there is a sameness to the symbols. Over and over, they trace the form of a fish, a peacock, or a vine, as if they were expressing some shared store of images, a collective imagination.

The first Christians traced those lines because they wanted them to stand forever as a perpetual prayer, for remembrance of the dead, for the perseverance of the living, and for deliverance in times of trial. And they were more than prayer: they were a proclamation, a telling of the good news in symbols that would speak to many people, regardless of literacy, regardless even of language. One of the lasting ways they bore witness to their Christian faith was in these symbols.

These signs sketch the basic grammar that Christians speak to one another across cultures and across millennia. The symbols that recur on vials and jars of the third century are the same symbols that turn up on the walls of our churches today.

Few of us today, however, can even begin to understand the messages left for us by our ancestors. We have lost our Christian mother

Bust of Christ with dolphins.
San Vitale presbytery mosaic, Ravenna, Italy. Sixth century.
For more about dolphin symbolism, see Chapter 8, The Dolphin.

tongue — the code of the martyrs — and we are impoverished by the loss. They have become like hieroglyphics, a language that only academic specialists understand. What is worse is that we have forgotten how to think the way these distant ancestors thought, and this has rendered them even more remote from us. Their symbols seem incomprehensible now.

Yet delivering the message was, for them, clearly an urgent matter, a matter of ultimate consequence. To carve or paint or scratch these symbols, they burrowed into the ground and breathed foul air while laboring in dim lamplight. Our ancestors did this so that their message might reach us. We owe them at least the effort of a sympathetic study.

⳨

And that is what this book is all about. It is a lexicon, but it is more than that. We have collected many instances of the symbols of the first four Christian centuries — the centuries of persecution and great doctrinal development — the period that scholars call "paleo-Christian." We have defined these symbols using, whenever possible, the words of the early Church. For this we have culled the sermons, rites, and letters of the Church Fathers and Mothers, but also the court records of their pagan persecutors and the broadsides of Christianity's most hostile enemies. For the Christians used symbols with remarkable consistency, whether they were chiseling them into the walls of their tombs, preaching them to a congregation, or addressing them to a cynical magistrate. All the ancient sources can help us, because the symbols we are studying emerged from a complex culture — a culture that the Christians kept for themselves, but that borrowed extensively from the broader culture in which they lived. Many of the early Christians, after all, were converts. They had been pagan or Jewish. Many, moreover, could not read. Thus, their "visual vocabulary" was an extremely important element in their religious experience. The early Christians borrowed freely from the symbols of pagans and Jews, but they gave each symbol a distinctively Christian meaning.

For the early Christians found themselves caught between worlds. Faith told them that a new heaven and a new earth, a new creation, had come in Jesus Christ. They lived in the same old world, but with a new vision. Those who weren't Jews (and many of them weren't) were told that they'd been incorporated into the family history of Israel. At their baptism, their bishop told them that they were now children of Abraham, liberated from slavery with Moses — because Jesus Himself was a son of Abraham, and Jesus Himself marked the definitive Passover. Israel's story and Israel's symbols were now the Church's. But all the symbols from

Metal ring with labarum. Ostia. Museo Ostiense, Italy.
For more labarum symbolism, see Chapter 25, The Labarum.

ancient Israel now had a new fullness of meaning. Thus, even the Jews who converted had to learn to read their symbolic heritage in a new light.

None of this was easy. How, after all, could a newly baptized man or woman, especially someone who had been pagan, cling to a common symbol without dragging its associated idols along with it? Sometimes it was a question of finding a symbol that would be appropriate on a family's signet ring, now that the family had rejected the old household or civic gods. The cultures of antiquity — whether Greek, Roman, or Persian — made no distinctions between the sacred and the secular, so the gods and their images were everywhere.

At the end of the second century, St. Clement of Alexandria addressed the problem in a very practical way. Christians, he said, should choose common symbols from the wider culture — but symbols that admitted of a Christian meaning, images that had equally strong associations with the Church's scripture, ritual, or tradition: "Let our seals be either a dove, or a fish, or a ship with its sails full of wind, or a musical lyre, which Polycrates used, or a ship's anchor, which Seleucus got engraved as a device. And if there should appear a fisherman, remember the apostle, and the children drawn out of the water. For we are not to draw the faces of idols, and we are forbidden to cling to them; nor should we use a sword or a bow, since we are peacemakers; nor drinking cups, since we are temperate."

The early Christians kept, more or less, within these limits. Yet, even with these constraints, they found an abundance of images at hand. Their first resource was the Bible, with its rich history and metaphor. The biblical images had for generations been stereotyped in the iconography of the synagogues of the Jews. Though later Judaism came to reject most religious artwork, the synagogues of late antiquity were lavishly decorated. In some we find biblical scenes — Jonah, Abraham, David — alongside purely symbolic figures, like the lamb, the lamp, the vine, and the fish. In the words of Joseph Ratzinger: "The Christian images, as we find them in the catacombs, simply take up and develop the canon of images already established by the synagogue, while giving it a new modality of presence."

In other words, the types had now found their fulfillment in the Church. The symbols no longer spoke merely of the past or the future, but signified an abiding reality, here and now.

In some cases, it is not clear whether the Christians are borrowing from Jewish precedents, or the Jews are borrowing from Christian precedents. Diaspora Judaism and catholic Christianity were both maturing at a rapid pace, within the same culture, and claiming the same roots. Both, moreover, felt increasingly free to borrow from pagan art forms.

We find a Christian justification for such borrowing as early as St. Justin Martyr (A.D. 150) and continuing through St. Clement of Alexandria and the later historian Eusebius of Caesaria. Since their God is the Lord of all history, they explained, He was active in pagan cultures as well, preparing the way for them to receive the Gospel someday. In the works of the philosophers, poets, and artists, he planted "seeds of the Word." Thus, St. Justin could argue that "whatever is true is ours." And Christian artists could feel a certain freedom in drawing from the symbols of paganism, just as Christian theologians felt free to borrow notions from Plato.

The Church, then, could appropriate the symbols of pagans and Jews and "baptize" them, putting them to Christian use. These symbols spoke the visual language of the people, many of whom were former pagans or former Jews, and many of whom, again, could not read.

☙

Our key to understanding the early-Christian use of symbols can be summed up in a single word: typology.

Typology is the discernment of "typical" patterns of God's activity throughout salvation history. The Greek word "typos" commonly denoted a physical impression, whether on metal, on paper, or on clay — the face on a coin, the stamp of a seal on a legal document, or a potter's trademark on the lamp he made. The type is something that recurs, something recognizable, a symbol that signifies a person who is the artist or craftsman.

The Catacombs of St. Sebastian, Rome.
For more anchor symbolism, see Chapter 23, The Anchor.

Typology recognizes the universe and all of history as belonging to God. He is their author, origin, and end; so everything in creation holds together in a single narrative design. **Everything that exists** expresses God's design, His pattern.

Old Testament typologies celebrate the great moments in God's plan — creation, the ark of Noah, the call of Abraham, the Passover, the kingdom of David — and hence everything associated with those moments is invested with extraordinary symbolic value: the lamb, the unleavened bread, Moses' staff, Noah's ark, David's livelihood as a shepherd.

Jesus Himself discerned the Old Testament's typological patterns, as did all the authors of the New Testament. St. Paul noted that "Adam . . . was a type of the one who was to come" (Rom 5:14). The First Epistle of St. Peter refers to baptism as an "antitype," that is, the thing signified by God's rescue of Noah (1 Pt 3:21). Indeed, Jesus presented Himself as the fulfillment of God's typical pattern. He was Himself the antitype, the thing signified, by all the former types: "And beginning with Moses and all the prophets, He interpreted to them in all the scriptures the things

Chapter 1: The Background   17

Long Lamp.
For more lamp symbolism, see Chapter 11, The Lamp.

concerning Himself" (Lk 24:27). God's hand was in every event of Israel's history, guiding people and events so that they would foreshadow or prefigure the definitive saving acts of Jesus Christ.

We can see Justin Martyr's appropriation of pagan culture as an extension of the typological approach, beyond Scripture, even to pagan culture. If God acted in the history of the Greeks — and, as Lord of History, surely He did — then He must have left seeds of His Word among the pagans. These, too, are "types" that Christians can discern and use profitably (though they are certainly of a far lower status than the biblical types).

We can see the same principle at work in the general tendency of the early Christians to adopt symbols from nature — such as the dolphin — or from the professions — the sailor or the farmer. St. Clement of Alexandria put it well: "If we accept salvation, then all things are ours without cost — earth, sea, heaven, and all things living in them. The creatures that fly and those that swim, all that is upon the earth is ours."

All Scripture, nature, and culture were fair game as religious symbols; because the God of the Christians is the Lord of all. Or, in the authoritative words of St. Paul to the first generation of Christians in Greece: "All things are yours . . . and you are Christ's; and Christ is God's" (1 Cor 3:21-23).

This is a foundational principle not only of early Christian symbology, but also of the spirituality of the Fathers. We hear it in the fifth-century prayer known as **St. Patrick's Breastplate**: "Christ with me, Christ before me, Christ behind me, Christ in me, Christ beneath me, Christ above me, Christ on my right, Christ on my left, Christ when I lie down, Christ when I sit down, Christ when I arise."

For Patrick, as for his near forebears in the faith, Christ was omnipresent in nature. For the faithful Christian reader, He was omnipresent, too, in Scripture, as Pope Damasus I (fourth century) demonstrated in a poem that merely catalogs the scriptural types and titles of Christ:

> *Hope, Road, Life, Health, Reason, Wisdom, Light,*
> *Judge, Gate, Giant, King, Gem, Prophet, Priest,*
> *Messiah, Sabbath, Rabbi, Spouse, Mediator,*
> *Branch, Pillar, Hand, Rock, Son, and Emmanuel,*
> *Vineyard, Shepherd, Sheep, Peace, Root, Vine, Olive,*
> *Fountain, Wall, Lamb, Calf, Lion, Propitiator,*
> *Word, Man, Net, Stone, House — Everything —*
> > *Christ Jesus!*

Aster inscription. Tombstone from the Monteverde catacomb, Rome.
For more about dove symbolism, see Chapter 16, The Dove.

What set Christian types and symbols apart from those of the pagans and Jews was what set Chistian life apart from other ways of life. Cardinal Ratzinger called the Christian difference a "new modality of presence" — and that new modality was, quite simply, the sacramental life of the Church. The artworks of the synagogues preserved a record of past events in the history of Judaism, even as they anticipated a future fulfillment. The artwork of the pagan shrines recounted the myths that claimed a certain timelessness.

But the art of nascent Christianity intended to "incorporate the events of history into the sacrament." What does that mean? It means that, by participating in the rites of the Church, each and every Christian was stepping into the stream of salvation history. Each was taking his or her place alongside Abraham, Moses, and David, Peter and Paul, and the martyrs. God's saving action was not a matter of the long-ago past or a vague and distant future, but a reality of the most immediate present — it was **really present**, and experienced in the baptismal water, the oil of anointing, and in the bread and wine of the liturgy. This is the overarching theme that runs through the vast array of symbols we find on the walls, lamps, rings, medals, cups, caskets, coins, and flasks of Christian antiquity.

This was more than theory, more than theology, more than the excitement of sharing a secret or cracking a code. St. Cyril of Jerusalem talked about the difference these symbols made in the everyday spirituality of ordinary Christians. "The Savior comes in different forms for the benefit of each person. To those who lack joy, He becomes a Vine; and to those who wish to enter, He stands as a Door. To those who need to offer up their prayers, He stands as a mediating High Priest. To those who have sins, He becomes a Sheep, that He may be sacrificed for them. He becomes all things to all men, keeping what He is in His own nature."

The lamb on the lamp, then, was a reminder of a truth at the heart of life — a truth worth dying for.

℘

We have tried in this book to provide a key to understanding not only the early Christian symbols, but the early Christians' **experience** of these symbols as well. We wanted to recover the freshness and urgency of the original images — to show the symbols as they first appeared and explain how they "worked," using the words of the early Christians themselves. This material will help to demonstrate the significance of each particular symbol in the life of the Church, in history, and in the lives of individual believers.

In depicting the symbols, we tried, again whenever possible, to model our illustrations on the real archeological remains of the era of the Fathers. We have, however, restored them to some semblance of their original condition — again, to enable modern readers to experience the symbols not as artifacts but as personal messages, from one Christian generation to another.

We have also tried to use words and images from the range of the early Christian world — not only the Roman orbit, as most other books on symbols do, but also the rich cultures of East Syrian and Coptic Christianity.

Some readers might wonder at the relative lengths of our chapters. Mostly this reflects the importance of a particular symbol in the culture of Christian antiquity, or the frequency with which it appears in the archeological record. Sometimes, however, we gave more attention to certain symbols simply because they have been relatively neglected in recent generations. Finally, in some instances, the size of the chapter merely reflects the idiosyncrasies of the author and illustrator.

෴

A symbol is, by definition, something that stands for or suggests something else. The relationship of the sign to the signified can be complex. It can arise from historical association, social convention, or mere physical resemblance. Sometimes several of these factors enter the equation.

Indeed, there is no shortage of books that treat the interpretation of

Early cryptogram. Graffito from the Catacombs of Domitilla, Rome.
For more anchor symbolism, see Chapter 23, The Anchor.

symbols like a sort of algebra: the fish = Jesus Christ; the ship = the Church; and so on. Such books are extremely valuable. But the meaning of symbols is rarely so simple. Sometimes a lone symbol stands for a multitude of realities: either the fish or the lamb can represent Jesus, or the individual believer, or the Eucharist that binds the Christian to Christ — or, most likely, it can represent all three at once. Often multiple symbols can stand for the same reality: as the fish, the lamb, and the shepherd all refer to Christ.

Thus in any book on symbols there will be much repetition. Yet each symbol has its own suggestive power, it own resonances, its own evocations of Scripture. Each symbol reflects a different aspect of some reality that many symbols hold in common. The Eucharist as mother's milk elicits a different response in the beholder than, say, the Eucharist as the Passover Lamb or the ubiquitous fish.

A twentieth-century scholar of ancient symbols, Erwin Goodenough, put the matter very well: "The symbols of Christianity . . . are indeed many. . . . Yet all of these will fit into a single formula, namely that the eternal God lovingly offers to share his nature with man, to lift him into eternal participation in divine life and happiness. Each symbol presents a facet of a single jewel."

That jewel is, for us moderns, too often a treasure hidden in a field (see Mt 13:44). It is up to each of us to buy back the treasures of Christian antiquity, not so much the relics themselves, but the things they stand for — the realities behind the symbols — the spirit of the Church's founding generations.

A symbology is a system of symbols, a kind of language. And a language, even a visual language, sets a kind of boundary for a people or a nation. It includes the natives (the baptized) and excludes the aliens (pagans). Recovering a common Christian language, we can recover a sense of the nearness of our ancestors, the immediacy of the family we call the Communion of Saints.

Ancient Sources:
- St. Clement of Alexandria, *The Teacher* 3.2.
- St. Clement of Alexandria, *Exhortation* 94.2.
- St. Justin Martyr, *Second Apology* 13.
- Pope St. Damasus I, *Epigrams* 50.
- St. Patrick, *Confessions*.
- St. Cyril of Jerusalem, *Catechetical Lectures* 10.5.

Modern Sources:
- Ratzinger, *Spirit* 117-118.
- Goodenough/Neusner, *Jewish Symbols* 56.

Chapter 2
The Fish

⸏

And wherever the river goes . . . there will be very many fish. . . .
Fishermen will stand beside the sea . . . its fish will be of very
many kinds, like the fish of the Great Sea.
Ezekiel 47:9-10

The fish is the symbol most commonly associated with the ancient Church. It is everywhere in the archeological record — scratched onto walls as graffiti, traced onto lamps, and detailed in beautiful mosaics and frescos. The Fathers left an impressive paper trail explicating the fish and its many layers of meaning, for the symbol was as complex as it was common.

The only symbol comparable, for modern believers, is the cross, which was itself rarely depicted in Christianity's earliest years. Today the cross appears on steeples and hymnals, necklaces and bumper stickers. The fish had a similar ubiquity in antiquity.

What did the fish represent? Above all, it was Jesus Christ. The dominant language of the early Church was Greek, and in Greek the phrase "Jesus Christ, Son of God, Savior" produced the acronym ICHTHYS, the Greek word for fish. A Christian poem of the second century spells the word with the first letters of each line. Thus, the fish is a simple creed: it professes belief in Jesus' divinity and His identity as the Christ, the anointed Savior (see Mt 16:16).

Scholars, however, believe that the visual symbol preceded the acronym. Fish are plentiful in the Scriptures that were proclaimed in the Church's liturgy, so the symbol evoked many scenes familiar from sacred history. Ezekiel's prophecy, cited above, was often interpreted as a vision of the future Church, whose baptismal "river" would be home to many "fish," that is, many Christians who are identified with Jesus Christ. Of

The Last Supper — Coptic plaque from the Church of Sts. Sergius and Bacchus.
The Coptic Museum, Cairo, Egypt.

The "Eucharistic fish" with the basket of bread and the cup of red wine.
The Catacombs of St. Callistus, Rome. Late second – early third century.

course, the fishermen who "stand beside the sea" foreshadow the apostles and their successors, the bishops, whom Jesus appointed as "fishers of men" (Mt 4:19).

The fish is Jesus, and the fish is also the individual believer. There is no contradiction here and no confusion. Writing in North Africa around A.D. 198, the Christian theologian Tertullian explained: "We little fishes, after the example of our fish, Jesus Christ, are born in water. Nor have we safety in any other way than by permanently abiding in water." Though he writes in Latin, Tertullian shifts to the Greek word *ichthys* when he describes Jesus. Surely he means his hearers to remember the acrostic "Jesus Christ, Son of God, Savior," which was by then firmly established in Christian culture.

Indeed, such fish symbolism may originate in the common patrimony of Christians and Jews. The prophet Habbakuk had said, "You have made man like the fish of the sea" (Hab 1:14); and, according to the Babylonian Talmud, Rabbi Samuel offered an interpretation strikingly similar to that of Tertullian, his Christian contemporary. "Men are compared with fishes," said the Jewish sage, "because just as fishes of the sea die at once when they come up on dry land, so does man also die as soon as he abandons the Torah and the precepts."

A Christian separated from the Church, like a Jew apart from the Torah, was a person out of his element — a fish out of water — condemned to spiritual death.

But we have not yet touched on the original and the deepest meaning of the fish. The fish is the primal symbol of the Holy Eucharist. One need not be Catholic to recognize this fact. Erwin Goodenough, an agnostic scholar at Yale University, wrote that the Gospel According to John — which he called "the primitive Gospel" — gives us "the earliest explicit acceptance of the fish as a eucharistic symbol and as a symbol of the Savior who was eaten in the Eucharist." John does this, in his sixth chapter, by moving immediately from Jesus' multiplication of the loaves and fishes to the Bread of Life discourse, His most famous eucharistic sermon. Jesus is the bread come down from heaven, multiplied for the multitude. At the end of John's Gospel, we see the figures of fish and bread return as Jesus prepares a lakeside meal for the disciples (Jn 21:9). For the early Christians, all of these events prefigured the life-giving blessing that Jesus bestowed upon the Church. The Protestant scholar of archeology Graydon Snyder concluded: "The fish was, with the bread, the primary symbol for the Eucharist, the meal that developed, maintained, and celebrated the new community of faith."

No text could make the association as clearly as one particular depiction in Rome's Catacomb of St. Callistus. There we see two fish on a gravestone, one fish bearing bread, the other bearing a cluster of grapes: the eucharistic bread, the eucharistic wine . . . and the symbolic eucharistic fish.

Fragment from Ichtys Zonton epitaph — Fish of the Living.
The Vatican necropolis (now in the Vatican Museum). Third century.

Fish taking Eucharist.
Epitaph from the Catacombs of St. Callistus, Rome. Third century.

Two famous tombstones speak of the fish in eucharistic terms. The first bears a twenty-two-line poem dictated by a bishop named Abercius, from Hieropolis in Phrygia (now part of Turkey), around the year A.D. 216. The poem is as allusive and symbolic as the paintings of the catacombs — encoded so that only a Christian could understand: "Faith was my guide, and set before me as nourishment the fish from the deep. Very large, very pure, this fish that the chaste virgin held in her arms; that she gave to its friends to eat everywhere, having excellent wine, giving it as a drink mixed with water, together with bread."

The second inscription is later and was excavated in Autun, France. Its age is uncertain, but its style corresponds to that of Abercius, using similarly cryptic language to describe the Eucharist. The gravestone exhorts the living to make the most of their Mass — to eat, drink, and be merry, in the most spiritual sense: "O divine race of the heavenly fish, with a respectful heart receive immortal life among mortals. Rejuvenate your soul, my friend, in divine waters, by wisdom's eternal streams, which give true riches. Receive the delicious nourishment of the Savior of the saints. Eat, drink, taking the fish with both hands."

There are many variations on the theme of the eucharistic fish. One eucharistic bread stamp, unearthed in Italy, shows a simple fish with the Greek word "lethe" (death) in its belly. And that fish speaks volumes. St. Paul wrote, in his great eucharistic treatise, his First Letter to the Corinthians: "Death is swallowed up in victory!" (1 Cor 15:54). He is alluding to an oracle of the prophet Isaiah: "He will swallow up death for ever, and the Lord God will wipe away tears from all faces, and the reproach of His people He will take away from all the earth" (Is 25:8). That was the work of the eucharistic "fish," the work of Jesus Christ, according to the understanding of St. Paul. It was this understanding that he passed on to his disciples in Rome, whose descendants in the Church marked their bread with the fish — the divine fish who swallowed up death.

The fish appears often in wall paintings that depict banquet scenes. It is possible that these images present a snapshot of the *agape* meal, the dinner that sometimes accompanied the Eucharist in the primitive Church (see 1 Cor 11). It is also possible that the paintings represent a Friday dinner of fish that was customary for Jews in antiquity — and remains customary for many Christians today. Most likely, however, these fish are symbols of the real presence of Jesus Christ in the Eucharist; even the Last Supper appears often as a fish dinner rather than a Passover meal. In fact, that is the way it appears in an ancient mosaic of the Last Supper, at Tabhga, near Capernaum — the very site in the Holy Land where Jesus multiplied the loaves and fishes.

A tile from Dura Europos. Syria. Around A.D. 240.

When Christians celebrated the Eucharist, they began a meal they hoped to enjoy for all eternity. A great poet of the ancient Church, St. Paulinus of Nola, described his vision of that heavenly banquet, and in doing so he brought together many of the meanings of the fish: "I see the gathering divided among separate tables, and all the people are filled with abundance of food, so that before their eyes there appears the plenty bestowed by the Gospel's blessing and the picture of those crowds whom Christ, the true Bread and the Fish of living water, filled with five loaves and two fishes."

The fish is a creed. It is baptismal. It is eucharistic. It is Christ. It is the Christian. By faith, by baptism, by the Eucharist, believers know communion with God. They are identified with Him, partakers of the divine nature (2 Pt 1:4) — little fish in the likeness of the big fish, who is Jesus Christ.

St. Ambrose of Milan bids us to linger in meditation upon nature's fish, and learn from them: "Imitate the fish, which . . . should fill you with wonder. It is in the sea, and above the waves. It is in the sea, and swims over the billows. In the sea the storm rages, the winds howl; but the fish swims, it does not sink, because it is wont to swim. To you, this world,

Tombstone graffito. The Catacombs of St. Sebastian, Rome.

Church floor mosaic from Megiddo. Galilee, Israel.

too, is a sea. It has many billows, heavy waves, fierce storms. Be a fish, so that the waves of the world do not sink you."

Ancient Sources:

- *R. Samuel, in **Babylonian Talmud, Abodah Zarah** 3b.*
- *Tertullian, **On Baptism** 1.*
- *St. Ambrose of Milan, **On the Sacraments** 3.1.3.*
- *St. Paulinus of Nola, **Letters** 13.11.*
- *St. Augustine, **Tractate on John** 123.2.*

Modern Sources:

- *Danielou, **Primitive Christian Symbols** 50-57.*
- *Goodenough, 5:33.*
- *Snyder, in Donfried and Richardson, 84.*
- *Aquilina, **Mass of the Early Christians** 115-117.*

Chapter 3
The Orant

ℐ

I desire then that in every place the men should pray,
lifting holy hands.
1 Timothy 2:8

The orant is perhaps the only ancient Christian symbol whose meaning has been officially defined in Catholic doctrine. In its discussion of the Eucharist as the Church's sacrifice, the **Catechism of the Catholic Church** declares: "In the catacombs the Church is often represented as a woman in prayer, arms outstretched in the praying position. Like Christ who stretched out His arms on the cross, through Him, with Him, and in Him, she offers herself and intercedes for all men" (n. 1368).

It is a good and compact definition, and it rests on solid evidence found in the art and writings of the first Christian centuries.

But the orant is not a symbol peculiar to Christianity. In the ancient world, stretching back centuries before Christ, it was a universal sign of prayer and piety; and it has been unearthed in Jewish and even pagan settings. It appears quite often, for example, on the coins and civic monuments of the Roman Empire, representing the virtue of *pietas*: the special reverence due to the family, the gods, and the homeland (or the state). And, of course, any reader of the Bible will frequently encounter the orant; for example, in Moses praying for victory in battle (Ex 17:11) and in David seeking deliverance in the Psalms (Ps 28:2).

The orant — some scholars prefer the Latin spelling, *orans*, or the French *orante* — is a robed figure, almost always female and usually veiled, who holds her hands upraised. The Latin word literally means "person at prayer."

Writing about A.D. 198, Tertullian assumed that the orant posture

Daniel between the two lions.
Detail from the Mas d'Aire Sarcophagus. Aire-sur-l'Adour, France. Around A.D. 270.

Female orant figure.
Detail from the Sarcophagus of the Via Lungara. Museo delle Terme, Rome. Before A.D. 313.

is the ordinary way that Christians pray, and he sees this as an image of the Savior. "We not only raise our arms, but even expand them. We imitate the Lord's passion, confessing Christ as we pray." Around the same time, Minucius Felix extended that reading to every praying figure, regardless of religion; for him, the mere pose was a sign of Christ crucified: "We assuredly see a natural sign of a cross . . . when a man adores a deity, with a pure mind and with hands outstretched."

Because most people prayed with arms outstretched, to pray, then, was to take on the image of Jesus Christ. In the fourth century, Ambrose brought the discussion back to St. Paul's words to Timothy, asking the newly baptized members of the Church of Milan: "What is meant by 'lifting holy hands'? Shouldn't you, in your prayer, show forth the cross of the Lord to everyone?" According to Ambrose's biographer, St. Paulinus of Nola, the great bishop died holding his arms outstretched.

The orant pose remained the normal and universal posture of prayer throughout the age of the Church Fathers. St. John Chrysostom, preaching some time between A.D. 398 and 403, noted that the entire congregation prayed this way during the eucharistic liturgy: "For when the whole people stands with uplifted hands, a priestly assembly, and that awe-inspiring sacrifice lies displayed, how shall we not prevail with God?"

Chrysostom makes an important connection. The orant pose is a priestly gesture. It is a posture appropriate for offering sacrifice to God. And the Catholic Church's priesthood, then as now, was not restricted to the clergy. As Scripture makes clear, all the faithful comprise "a nation of priests" (1 Pt 2:9; see also Rev 1:5-6 and 5:9-10). The laity share in the priestly office of Jesus Christ, who alone is the true and eternal high priest. The lay members of the early Church were keenly aware of their common priesthood and the special role they played in the holy sacrifice of the Mass.

The fiery furnace.
Detail from a sarcophagus found near St. Sebastian, Rome (now in the Vatican Museum).

Noah. Fresco from the Catacombs of Sts. Peter and Marcellinus, Rome. Fourth century.

Epitaph of Irene.
The Catacombs of St. Callistus, Rome. Third century.

In the Egyptian Liturgy of St. Mark, the sacrificial portion of the rite — the Eucharistic Prayer — begins with the deacon calling out to the congregation: "Stretch out your arms."

Thus, the orant was not merely an artistic prop. It was a sight seen in ordinary life.

Yet it is everywhere in the artistic record as well. The orant is the human figure most commonly found in the art and decorations of the ancient Church. Since it often appears on funerary art, at gravesites and on sarcophagi, some scholars believe that the orant sometimes represents the soul of the dead. "Soul" is a feminine noun in many ancient languages, and this might explain why the figure is almost always portrayed as female.

Other interpreters believe that the orant symbolizes a Christian in mortal peril, praying to heaven for deliverance. This hypothesis might

Vitalia in pace.
Fresco from the Catacombs of Januarius, Naples, Italy. After A.D. 400.

help us to explain the orant's gradual decline in popularity during the centuries after the large-scale persecutions had ceased.

At times the orant appears as a character in the depiction of a biblical scene. Amid the lions, Daniel stands with arms outstretched. Amid the flames, the three holy children stand as orantes. Jonah stands in the same pose as he faces the great fish, and Noah as the flood waters rise. Often, however, even these male figures appear with feminine features and clothing. Perhaps the images represent their souls at prayer.

Similarly, if we follow the **Catechism** in seeing the orant as the Church, the feminine aspect would make sense. The Fathers spoke of the Church as "mother"; and the Scriptures speak of the Church as Christ's "bride." Thus, the image of the Church at prayer, like the image of the individual soul at prayer, should naturally be feminine.

And it is not heresy, in a book on symbolism, to wonder whether realism played a part in these depictions. In the age of the Fathers, as in our own age, women usually outnumbered men in any given congregation.

In later centuries, other gestures and poses became more customary in the practice of prayer, and so became more common as artistic symbols of prayer. But the orant posture never disappeared. It has endured as a devotional practice, used especially with the Stations of the Cross, in

Belgium, Holland, and Germany. It emerged again, at the mid-twentieth century, in the prayer groups of the Catholic Charismatic Renewal. And it has always been a common pose of the priest during the Mass. There is something timeless about its suggestive power, as even the words of the Mass attest: "He stretched out His arms between heaven and earth in the everlasting sign of Your covenant" (Eucharistic Prayer for Masses of Reconciliation I).

Ancient Sources:
- *Tertullian, **On Prayer** 14; see also his **Apology** 30.*
- *Minucius Felix, **Octavius** 29.*
- *St. Ambrose of Milan, **On the Sacraments** 6.18.*
- *Chyrsostom, **Homilies on Philippians** 3.4.*
- *Paulinus, **Life of Ambrose** 10.47.*

Modern Sources:
- *Jungmann, 1:239.*
- *Snyder, 35-38.*
- *Jensen, **Understanding** 35-37.*

Chapter 4
The Shepherd

I am the good shepherd;
I know my own and my own know me.
John 10:14

The figure of the shepherd emerges with the first instances of Christian art, and it dominates the archeological record. Well over a hundred Christian images of the shepherd have survived in the Roman catacombs alone, in engravings, fresco paintings, sarcophagi, and free-standing sculpture. They depict the shepherd in a wide variety of poses: with a lamb slung over his shoulder, with musical instruments, with a milking pail, amidst his flock.

They are all, of course, images of Jesus, who called Himself the Good Shepherd (Jn 10:11-16).

But they are symbolic representations, not portraits. Jesus, after all, was a craftsman by trade, not a herdsman. When He spoke of Himself as a shepherd, He spoke metaphorically, choosing a powerful metaphor with a long history. Indeed, few images have such a rich biblical pedigree, in both the Old and New Testaments. In the Hebrew Scriptures, "shepherd" is a favored metaphor for God and for the king of Israel. It appears as early as the Book of Genesis, where Jacob describes the Lord as "the Shepherd, the Rock of Israel" (Gen 49:24). It is an especially apt metaphor for Israel's monarch, since the founder of the dynasty, David, received his royal anointing while he was still a shepherd boy.

As the Son of God and the Son of David, Jesus had a dual claim to the title of shepherd, and He applied it to Himself (Mt 26:31 and Mk 6:34, for example). The first generation of Christians did so as well (see Heb 13:20; 1Pt 2:25; Rev 7:17).

For the early Christians, Psalm 23 (22 in the Greek Septuagint Bible) became the great source of images of the Good Shepherd:

The Good Shepherd.
Fresco from the Catacombs of St. Callistus — Crypts of Lucina, Rome. Third century.

GERONTI VIBAS IN DEO — Gerontius, live in God.
Funerary inscription. Museo Lateranense, Rome. End of third century.

The Lord is my shepherd, I shall not want;
He makes me lie down in green pastures.
He leads me beside still waters;
He restores my soul . . .
Even though I walk through the valley of the shadow of
    death,
I fear no evil;
 for You are with me . . .
You prepare a table before me
in the presence of my enemies;
You anoint my head with oil,
 my cup overflows. . . .
I shall dwell in the house of the Lord forever.

In these lines, homilists and artists found vivid models for their work. Like the images of the Good Shepherd in the catacombs, the commentaries on Psalm 23 are plentiful in the works of the Church Fathers. In fact, there is a remarkable correspondence between the literary record and the pictorial record, even in the allegorical details. The Fathers interpreted "the house of the Lord" to mean the Church, and we find this vividly portrayed in a fresco in Rome's Catacombs of Priscilla. There, Christ appears as a shepherd; and His image is flanked by ecclesiastical figures — a bishop giving the veil to a consecrated virgin, orant figures, and so on.

From these early years, Christians viewed their bishops also as shepherds, who received their office from Christ. This was especially true of St. Peter, whom Christ designated as Rock (Mt 16:18), and to whom He delegated the role of Good Shepherd on earth (Jn 21:17). In evoking the shepherd and the rock, Jesus recalled the divine attributes from Jacob's blessing in Gen 49, thus bestowing special authority on His earthly vicar. It is not surprising that the image of the Good Shepherd appeared abun-

The Good Shepherd as Orpheus.
Detail from the Sarcophagus of Cyriacus, Ostia, Italy.

The Good Shepherd. Detail from the Sarcophagus of the Three Shepherds.
Museo Lateranense, Rome. End of third century.

dantly in Rome, which Christians have always honored as the locus of Peter's authority and the site of his martyrdom.

If the Shepherd's "green pastures" were the Church, then His "still waters," His "table," and His "oil" of anointing were the Church's sacraments. This was the Fathers' common reading of Psalm 23. "He leads them from pastoral meadows to the water of peace," said Origen in the third century, "and afterwards to the spiritual food and to the mysterious sacraments." Significantly, the Good Shepherd image appears in most of the early baptisteries; and Tertullian reports that it was a common decoration on liturgical vessels in the late seond century.

As a Psalm of King David, Psalm 23 brings together the pastoral, royal, ritual, and even musical themes that would ever be associated with the Good Shepherd. At one town in modern Syria, archeologists recently discovered a Christian church and a Jewish synagogue. In both were prominent images of a shepherd: in the synagogue, it was David; in the church, it was Jesus.

As the literary tradition of the shepherd was familiar to Jews, so the artistic renderings were familiar even to pagans. Both Jews and Christians seem to have adapted the visual image from very ancient Greek models. The Christian and Jewish portrayals of Jesus and David are indistinguishable from pagan images of Hermes (the divine protector of flocks) and Orpheus (the god of music and poetry). Hermes appears frequently in pastoral scenes, with a sheep or ram slung across his shoulders or a staff in his hand. Orpheus appears with a musical instrument, usually pipes or a lyre, because his songs were reputed to tame wild beasts.

The Church Fathers noted these similarities, but were careful to make distinctions. Indeed, Origen held that the pagan gods were "bad shepherds," fallen angels who set themselves up as illegitimate pastors of the nations. Christ, however, tamed believers with a new song (Rev 5:9, 14:3) that was true. Clement of Alexandria imagined the comparison with Orpheus coming from the mouth of Christ Himself: "But not such is My song, which has come to loose, and speedily, the bitter bondage of tyrannizing demons . . . [My song] alone has tamed men, the most intractable of animals. . . . This is the New Song, the manifestation of the Word that was in the beginning, and before the beginning."

After the peace of Constantine, the Church historian Eusebius records that the Good Shepherd image suddenly appeared everywhere — and now in the most public places. Even "the fountains in the marketplace" were "graced with figure of the Good Shepherd."

Eusebius continued to tease out the comparison between Christ and Orpheus: "The Greek myth tells us that Orpheus had power to charm ferocious beasts. He could tame their savage spirit by striking the chords of his instrument with a master hand. This story is celebrated by the Greeks. They generally believe that the power of melody, from an unconscious instrument, could subdue the savage beast and draw the trees from their places. But the author of perfect harmony is the all-wise Word of God, and He wanted to apply every remedy to the many afflictions of human

The Good Shepherd graffito. Detail from the Epitaph of a small girl, Apuleia Crysopolis, dedicated by her parents. The Catacombs of St. Callistus, Rome. Third century.

souls. So He employed human nature — the workmanship of His own wisdom — as an instrument, and by its melodious strains he soothed, not merely the brute creation, but savages endowed with reason, healing each furious temper, each fierce and angry passion of the soul, both in civilized and barbarous nations, by the remedial power of his Divine doctrine."

Pagans revered Orpheus also as a guide to the underworld. It was he who escorted the souls of the dead to their destiny. And so he appears on many tombs and in other funerary art. The early Christians eagerly took up these images as well, since there could be no better guide in the afterlife than their own Good Shepherd. Thus, in the catacombs, the figure of the shepherd is sometimes surrounded not only by sheep, but by praying orant figures as well.

Like Hermes and Orpheus, the shepherd Jesus always appears as a youth, hardly more than a boy, though strong in shoulders and limbs. He is beardless and short-haired, in contrast to the other symbolic images of Christ — the amply bearded philosopher, for example. As the shepherd boy, he exudes strength, joy, and eternal youth. It is a visual echo of the Church's early liturgies, such as those in the **Didache** and the **Apostolic Tradition**, which speak of Jesus as a child-servant (in Greek, **pais**). These, in turn, echo the apostolic preaching as it was recorded in the Acts of the Apostles; there the word **pais** turns up repeatedly as a title for Jesus. In Acts 4:30, for example, Peter and John apply the word to Jesus; while, interestingly enough, just five lines earlier (v. 25) they had applied it to David — the boy-shepherd who became the shepherd-king.

The young herdsman represents an approachable Savior. It is an image that does not pull rank. The shepherd wears the rough clothing, the short tunic, of a laborer. As a poor youth, He has no social status. His expression is often warm and welcoming. It is not surprising that, in two of the earliest reported apparitions of Jesus, He appeared to the Christian visionaries — St. Perpetua in Africa and Hermas in Rome — as a shepherd.

Many scholars believe that the shepherd image underwent a radical transformation before falling from ubiquitous prominence to relative

Jesus as the Good Shepherd.
A mosaic from the Mausoleum of Galla Placidia, Ravenna, Italy. Around A.D. 450.

obscurity. In the mausoleum of Galla Placida at Ravenna, Jesus appears as the Good Shepherd — but with a difference. Now, some two centuries after Christianity's triumph over paganism, Christ holds a golden cross in place of His shepherd's crook, and He is dressed in the finery of an emperor: gold and purple.

It is a shift in emphasis, but no less true. The persecuted Church looked to the shepherd Son of David for deliverance. The triumphant Church looked to the shepherd Son of God for its preservation and care.

In the Catholic Church — the Galla Placida mosaic seems to say — the Davidic shepherd has gathered the scattered tribes of the earth into one holy nation; and now, like David, He rules that nation as a shepherd-king.

Ancient Sources:

- *Origen, **Commentary on the Song of Songs**.*
- *Tertullian, **On Modesty** 10.*
- *St. Clement of Alexandria, **Exhortation to the Greeks** 1.*
- *Eusebius, **In Praise of Constantine** 14.*
- *Eusebius, **The Death of Constantine** 3.49.*
- *__Didache__ 9.*
- *St. Hippolytus of Rome, **Apostolic Tradition** 4.*

- *Martyrdom of Perpetua and Felicity.*
- *Hermas, **Shepherd** 1.5.*

Modern Sources:

- *Danielou, **Bible** 186-190.*
- *Finaldi, 11-12.*
- *Finegan, 383-385.*
- *Jensen, **Understanding** 37-41.*

Chapter 5
The Vine

⌁

I am the true vine, and my Father is the vinedresser . . .
I am the vine, you are the branches.
He who abides in me, and I in him, he it is that bears much
fruit, for apart from me you can do nothing.
John 15:1, 5

The vine, like many other symbols discussed in this book, was not exclusively Christian. It adorns the walls of Jewish synagogues and pagan shrines. The vine served as a symbol of the chosen people, Israel, and of Dionysos (Bacchus), the god of wine and pleasure. It was also a common decorative motif, void of any meaning other than the beauty of its winding tendrils.

The Bible is, of course, shot through with references to vines, vineyards, and the fruit of the vine — meaning grapes or their fermented product, wine. Some references to vines are literal, as in the case of Naboth, whose vineyard was coveted by King Ahab (1 Kings 21). Often, however, the prophets use the vine and the vineyard as a symbol or allegory of Israel. The most famous of these is Isaiah's "Song of the Vineyard" (Is 5:1-7):

> *My beloved had a vineyard*
>   *on a very fertile hill.*
> *He digged it and cleared it of stones,*
>   *and planted it with choice vines;*
> *he built a watchtower in the midst of it,*
>   *and hewed out a wine vat in it;*
> *and he looked for it to yield grapes,*
>   *but it yielded wild grapes . . .*

The Draught of Life.
Detail from a stone transenna, St. Apollinare Nuovo, Ravenna, Italy. Sixth century.

And now I will tell you
what I will do to my vineyard . . .
I will break down its wall,
and it shall be trampled down . . .
For the vineyard of the Lord of hosts
is the house of Israel,
and the men of Judah
are His pleasant planting;
and He looked for justice,
but behold, bloodshed;
for righteousness,
but behold, a cry!

The Prophet here foretells a catastrophe: the dissolution of the nation and the dispersion of the tribes of Israel, conquered by Assyria and exiled by Babylon, the line of King David apparently snuffed out. Jeremiah (5:10) and Ezekiel (19:12) also speak of these events in terms of the destruction of a vineyard.

Grapes and wine are suggestive of blood; and these were indeed

The Fruits of Paradise.
The Catacombs of St. Sebastian, Rome. Third century.

bloody events. Wine was colloquially known as "the blood of the grape" (see, for example, Gen 49:11). When Isaiah speaks of the coming judgment, he portrays God in red-stained apparel, His "garments like his that treads in the wine press" (Is 63:2). But it is the blood of wicked men that stains His clothes. The New Testament concludes with a reprise of these very images of God's judgment (Rev 14:19-20 and 19:15).

Yet the destruction and dispersion are tragic because Israel is God's beloved vineyard. The gathering of the scattered tribes was to be the great work of the expected Messiah-King.

At the time of Jesus' birth, the vine may have been a symbol of the integrity of the kingdom of Israel under the rule of the house of David. Herod the Great, who was not a Jew by birth, longed for royal legitimacy and was fearful of the emergence of a true Davidic heir. Herod had reconstituted many of the lands of old Israel, and he had begun the rebuilding of the Jerusalem Temple. He ordered his coins struck with a grapevine on their reverse side; he placed golden grapevines at the entrance to the Temple.

Jesus, too, took up the metaphor in a stirring parable, echoing the details of Isaiah's song — the vineyard, the hedge, the pit for the wine press, and the tower (Mk 12:1ff). For the Son of David, then, as for the pretender, the vine was a symbol of Israel, God's beloved.

But Jesus' most powerful evocation of the vine comes when He takes

Iulianus epitaph.
Inscription from the Catacombs of Monteverde, Rome.

The Source of Life.
Relief from a chancel slab, St. Apollinare Nuovo, Ravenna, Italy. Sixth century.

it as His own identity: "I am the true vine" (Jn 15:1). The early Christians pondered this statement; and, keenly aware of their own Jewish roots, they expressed many layers of meaning that we might miss.

The Jewish-Christian document called the **Didache** contains the earliest eucharistic texts that have survived, apart from the New Testament. Some scholars believe that the liturgical texts in the **Didache** were composed no later than A.D. 48 — which would make them older than most of the New Testament books.

The **Didache** evokes the vine in its prayer over the chalice of wine: "Now concerning the Eucharist, give thanks in this way. First, concerning the cup: 'We thank You, our Father, for the holy vine of David Your servant, which You made known to us through Jesus Your servant; to You be the glory for ever.'"

This is history's earliest surviving record of the phrase "vine of David." The traditional Jewish blessing over a cup of wine uses words that are similar to those of the Mass as we know it today: "Blessed are you, O God, our Lord, King of the Universe, creator of the fruit of the vine." In the **Didache**, however, the Christian assembly thanks God for the "vine of David," which Jesus has revealed.

It seems that the vine revealed through Jesus was somewhat different from the vine expected in the popular imagination. The Prophets had foretold the vine in a shadowy way; but "the true vine" is "the holy vine of David . . . made known to us through Jesus Christ."

Jesus revealed the kingdom of David, but not merely by reconstituting the vineyard of Israel. In the Old Testament the vine was Israel. In the New Testament it is Christ; He is the renewed Israel, and all believers — both Israelites and Gentiles — are incorporated in Him through their sharing in the eucharistic fruit of the vine, the eucharistic blood of the grape. In fact, he revealed the kingdom with His very action of instituting the Eucharist. At the Last Supper, He said to His apostles: "I assign to you, as My Father assigned to Me, a kingdom, that you may eat and drink at My table in my kingdom" (Lk 22:29-30).

From the **Didache** onward, the phrase "vine of David" echoes in the works of the Church Fathers. St. Clement of Alexandria wrote: "It is He [Jesus] who has poured out the wine, the blood of the vine of David, upon our wounded souls." Clement's immediate successor in the Alexandrian school, Origen, wrote: "We are inebriated with the blood of the true vine, which ascends from the root of David."

This vine was not confined to Palestine, but spread out through all the earth. Said Justin Martyr, around A.D. 155: "For the vine planted by God and Christ the Savior is His people." And the kingdom is universal, for the people are everywhere. A third-century liturgical document, the

Fragment from a Coptic frieze. Coptic Museum, Cairo. Fourth century.

Mosaic from the Church of the Ark. Tel Shiloh, West bank, Israel. Around A.D. 390.

Didascalia Apostolorum, further identified "God's planting" with "the holy vineyard of His Catholic Church."

Aphrahat the Persian Sage recognized this and praised God for giving the vineyard of the kingdom over to the least likely of earthly powers: "For Christ is the vineyard, and His Father is the husbandman; and they who drink of His cup are the vines. . . . And at His coming He handed over the kingdom to the Romans . . . and these children of Esau will keep the kingdom for its giver."

It is hardly surprising, then, that the vine, the vineyard, and clusters of grapes became a favorite decoration of Christian homes, tombs, and places of worship. The vine defined the Church, whether universal or domestic; and the Church was the eucharistic kingdom revealed through Jesus Christ.

"Blessed is the vineshoot that became the cup of our salvation," sang St. Ephrem of Syria in one of his Christmas hymns. "Blessed also is the cluster, the source of the medicine of life."

This is the vine foretold to Israel. It is Christ. It is His people gathered in Him. It is His Church.

Like a vine I caused loveliness to bud,
and my blossoms became glorious and abundant fruit . . .
Come to me, you who desire me,
and eat your fill of my produce.
For the remembrance of me is sweeter than honey,
and my inheritance sweeter than the honeycomb.
Those who eat me will hunger for more,
and those who drink me will thirst for more. *(Sir 24:17,*
19-21; emphasis added)

Ancient Sources:
- *Didache 9.1-4.*
- *St. Clement of Alexandria, The Rich Man's Salvation 29.*
- *Origen, On Judges 6.*
- *Didascalia Apostolorum 1.*
- *St. Aphrahat, Demonstrations 5.22.*
- *St. Justin Martyr, Dialogue with Trypho 110.4.*
- *St. Ephrem, Hymns on the Nativity 3.15.*

Modern Sources:
- *Danielou, Primitive Christian Symbols 25-41.*
- *Murray, 95-130.*
- *Mazza, Origins 36-38.*
- *Mazza, Celebration 75-77.*
- *Goodenough 5:99-111; 6:128-141.*
- *Neusner 262, 657-658.*
- *Hahn, "Kingdom" 311-315.*

Chapter 6
The Philosopher

☙

*The beginning of wisdom is the most sincere desire for
instruction ... and love of her is the keeping of her laws ...
the desire for wisdom leads to a kingdom.*
Wisdom 6:17-18, 20

Philosophy means "the love of wisdom," and the ancients believed that such love could be pursued beyond the confines of academic institutions. The term "philosophy" could be used to describe religions, and indeed it was.

A pagan intellectual might survey the world's many sects and cults and assign each as a "philosophy" or a "superstition," basing all decisions on his individual tastes and prejudices. Pliny the Elder, a first-century naturalist, classified as "philosophers" both the Jewish sect of the Therapeutai and the faraway holy men of India. But the practices of the Chaldean Magi he deemed "superstition." He seems to have been unaware of Christianity, which was just arising in his lifetime; but his nephew, also named Pliny, was keenly aware of the new religious movement. And Pliny the Younger did not hesitate to condemn Christianity as "a depraved superstition carried to excess."

The standards, however, were somewhat arbitrary, and other pagan thinkers disagreed. For the great medical philosopher Galen, Christianity was "not inferior" to the established schools of philosophy.

Some Christians were eager to make the same case — and even take it a step further. Christian intellectuals, especially the apologists of the second and third centuries, strove to show that Christianity was the pinnacle of philosophy, and Jesus the perfect philosopher.

Christian art reflects these efforts. The visual figure of the philoso-

Christ teaching.

Ivory diptych from Murano, Italy. Museo Archeologico Nazionale, Ravenna. Sixth century.

Jesus as Philosopher.
Fresco from the Catacombs of Domitilla, Rome. Around A.D. 325.

pher, like that of the orant, followed a certain almost-universal stereotype in the ancient world. The wise man was seated, usually holding a scroll, and sometimes wearing the *pallium*, which was the traditional, distinctive garment of philosophers. Public figures were portrayed this way when the artist wanted to emphasize the wisdom of his human subject. A statue in the philosophical pose was a common way to flatter the emperor.

Christ appears as a philosopher in several sarcophagus carvings and catacomb paintings. He is usually surrounded by attentive disciples, as any wandering philosopher would be; in at least one portrayal, we see a disciple bowing low in adoration.

Saints and biblical figures, especially Moses and the apostles, also emerge in the pose of philosopher. A famous third-century statue of St. Hippolytus was recovered headless and restored in the nineteenth century, according to the type of the philosopher — unmistakably male, bald, and bearded. Some art historians, however, believe that the original was a female figure, an allegory not of the philosopher, but of *philosophy*, which was always portrayed as feminine.

How was Christianity like philosophy? Justin counts the ways: It leads to virtue and happiness; it concerns itself with fundamental moral questions, such as the existence of free will, as well as metaphysical questions, such as creation *ex nihilo*. Moreover, it inspires people to place high principle over human comfort or convenience — and even over life itself.

As Socrates was willing to die for the sake of truth, so was Jesus, and so were the Christian martyrs.

Some Christian intellectuals imitated Christ by pursuing the path of the philosopher. St. Justin Martyr, who in his youth had studied with Platonists, Aristotelians, and Pythagoreans, continued to wear the philosopher's garb, the *pallium*, even after his conversion. When he moved to Rome, he presented himself as a philosopher and gathered a school at his residence by the public baths. Justin spoke of the Old Testament prophets as philosophers, and of Christianity as the "crown" of philosophy.

In the next generation, Minucius Felix, a legal scholar and Roman judge, discussed Christianity with his colleagues as an exalted ethical system, the greatest in history.

Around the same time, St. Clement of Alexandria said: "What is Plato but Moses speaking Greek?"

The Sermon on the Mount.
Fragment of a sarcophagus. Museo delle Terme, Rome. Around A.D. 300.

Statue of St. Hippolytus. Museo Lateranense, Rome. Third century.

Tertullian, however, was ambivalent about philosophy. One of his often-quoted lines is "What has Athens to do with Jerusalem?" — meaning, "What has Greek philosophy to do with Israelite faith?" In his massive ***Apology***, he seems to place the term "philosopher" in direct opposition to the term "Christian," accusing pagan thinkers of pride, idolatry, sexual misbehavior, and even theft! Yet he also wrote a little essay titled ***On the Pallium***, in which he defends the wearing of the distinctive vestment, since it can avail Christian "philosophers" of a public hearing: "A philosopher, in fact, must be seen in order to be heard." If Athens has now to do with Jerusalem, it is a boon granted to Athens — and all to the glory of Jerusalem. "Rejoice, Pallium, and exult!" he wrote "A better philosophy has now deigned to honor you, since you have begun to be a Christian's garment."

When Christian culture prevailed, the Church continued using the

Jesus passing the law to St.Peter and St.Paul.
The Traditio Legis Sarcophagus, detail. Musee Reattu, Arles, France. Around A.D. 380.

philosopher's **pallium** as a liturgical vestment. It survives today as the sign of the office of a metropolitan archbishop. It survives as well in the art, and the wisdom, of the age of the Fathers and martyrs.

Ancient Sources
- *Pliny the Elder,* **Natural History** *5.18; 7.1; 30.*
- *Pliny the Younger,* **Letters** *10.96.*
- *St. Justin Martyr,* **Dialogue with Trypho** *1.2, 2.13, 7.1, 8.2, 9.2, 110.3.*
- *St. Clement of Alexandria,* **Tapestries** *1.22.150(1).*
- *Minucius Felix,* **Octavius.**
- *Tertullian,* **On the Prescription of Heretics** *7;* **On the Pallium** *6;* **Apology** *46.*

Modern Sources
- *Lampe, 100-103, 257-284.*

Chapter 7
The Phoenix

⌡

The Spirit of the Lord God is upon me, because the Lord has
anointed me . . . to grant to those who mourn in Zion . . . a
garland instead of ashes.
Isaiah 61:1, 3

The mythic phoenix, or firebird, was an elusive animal. The most critical ancient scholars (Herodotus, Pliny, Tacitus) believed in its existence, though none of them had ever seen one. Tacitus tells us that the phoenix's appearance in A.D. 39 was the talk of Rome's chattering classes.

The ancients uniformly believed, and on good testimony, that the phoenix lived far, far away. To those in Europe, the bird lived in Arabia. To those in Egypt, it lived in India. And so on.

All the ancient peoples knew about the phoenix. The Israelites did, and the bird appears in the Bible at least once or twice. As Job ponders his troubles, he says, "In my own nest I shall grow old; I shall multiply years like the phoenix" (Job 29:18). Some modern translations render the last word as "sand" — which is a valid alternative reading of the Hebrew — but it also renders the line meaningless. The ancient rabbis favored the phoenix instead.

Job is remembering more optimistic days when he could always imagine a return to vigor. This brings to his mind the legendary bird that lives five hundred years, then dies in glorious flames, only to rise up again from the ashes. This resurrection is the phoenix's only mode of reproduction.

The Greek word for phoenix is no less troublesome than the Hebrew. For *phoinix* can mean either the self-renewing bird — or the common date-palm tree. Tertullian read Psalm 92:12 in the Greek Bible (the

The phoenix. Detail from a floor mosaic in a country villa in Daphne, Syria (now in Louvre, Paris). Fifth century.

The phoenix graffito.
The Catacombs of St. Callistus, Rome. Third century.

Septuagint) as "The righteous flourish like the phoenix." That is, he said, they "revive from death, from the grave — to teach you to believe that a bodily substance may be recovered even from the fire. Our Lord has declared that we are 'of more value than many sparrows' (Mt 10:31). Well, if not better than many a phoenix too, it were no great thing. But must men die once for all, while birds in Arabia are sure of a resurrection?"

The phoenix arose early in Christian art and literature. St. Clement of Rome, writing in the late first century, called the phoenix a "wonderful sign" of the resurrection. And so it appears often near burial places — but also on lamps and other household items. The firebird is the subject of a long poem from the third or fourth century that is usually attributed to the Church historian Lactantius. It is not overtly Christian, though medieval scholars believed it to be a rich and subtle allegory of the life of Jesus Christ.

Almost everywhere in Christian antiquity, the phoenix stands for resurrection. Only in Rufinus is the bird's asexual reproduction introduced in support of Mary's virginal conception of Jesus. "Why should it be thought marvelous for a virgin to conceive, when it is well known that the Eastern bird, which they call the phoenix, is also born in this way — or reborn — without the intervention of a mate, that it remains continually one, and continually by being born or reborn succeeds itself?"

An old Jewish legend held that, when Eve offered all the animals a taste of the forbidden fruit, the phoenix was the only one to refuse her. For this, God rewarded it with eternal life. The apocryphal visions of Enoch report that the phoenixes dwell amid the cherubim, high in heaven.

A Syrian manual of church order from the mid-fourth century, the **Apostolic Constitutions**, draws the great lesson for Christians, ancient and modern: "If resurrection is proved by means of an irrational bird — as even [the Stoics] say — why do they foolishly dismiss our claims, when we profess that He who has the power to create everything out of nothing, also has the power to restore the human body, and raise it up again after its decay?"

Unlike the scientists of two thousand years ago, we know that the phoenix was only a fable. But, like our Christian ancestors, we treasure the story of the phoenix as a sign of a greater story — the greatest ever told.

———

Ancient Sources:

- *Herodotus,* **Histories** *2.73.*
- *Tacitus,* **Annals** *6.28.*
- *Pliny* **Natural History** *10.2.*
- **Genesis Rabbah** *19:5.*
- **Midrash Samuel** *12.*
- **Septuagint,** *Psalm XCI.12.*
- *Tertullian,* **On the Resurrection of the Flesh** *13.*
- *St. Clement of Rome,* **To the Corinthians** *25.*
- *Lactantius,* **The Phoenix.**
- *Rufinus,* **Commentary on the Apostles' Creed** *11.*
- **Apostolic Constitutions** *5.7.*
- **2 Enoch** *19.6.*

Modern Sources:

- *Ginzberg, 17.*
- *Lampe, 212.*

Coin from Antioch, Syria. A.D. 348–350.

Chapter 8

The Dolphin

∽

You dolphins and all water creatures, bless the Lord;
praise and exalt Him above all forever.
Daniel 3:79 (Confraternity Version)

Ancient mariners and people who inhabited coastal lands attributed human and even superhuman qualities to the dolphin. For that matter, so do their modern counterparts. It is not so long since a dolphin was the star of a popular dramatic television series.

When dolphins look up from the water, they seem to smile, to communicate. In antiquity, the dolphin was known as "the sailor's friend," a guide to lead ships out of troubled waters to safe harbor. Sea lore records many legends of dolphins rescuing drowning men and bearing them to shore. Captains considered dolphins an omen of good fortune. In Greek myth, the god Apollo, when he was bidden, became incarnate as a dolphin to intervene in earthly affairs. The name of the most popular shrine of Apollo's oracle, Delphi, may have derived from the Greek word for dolphin.

Aristotle marveled at the speed of dolphins moving through the sea. And pagan peoples throughout the world sketched the dolphin as a symbol on tombs and grave markers. The graceful sea mammal bore the souls of the beloved dead on its back, speeding on to the afterlife.

Jews in antiquity were just as fond of the dolphin. In the first century, Philo told the story of a boy who forged a lasting friendship with a dolphin. When the boy died young, the dolphin died of grief. The Babylonian Talmud cites a rabbi who called dolphins "humans of the sea." In the ruins of the third-century synagogue at Dura Europos, archeologists found fifteen ceiling tiles depicting dolphins.

Dolphin bearing a cross. Limestone fragment from the Coptic cemetery at Armant, Egypt (now in Louvre, Paris). Fourth–fifth century.

Dolphin wrapped around a trident.
Vault painting from the Catacombs of Villa Torlonia, Rome. Fourth century.

Christian sailors likened Jesus Christ to the dolphin. Pastoral images of the lamb were remote from their experience. But they knew countless stories of dolphins as rescuers, guides, and friends. As the dolphins appeared in the ancient legends, so Jesus served in life: rescuer, guide, and friend.

Dolphins appear frequently on the walls of the catacombs. As symbols of Christ, they bear the souls of the saints to glory. Sometimes they appear crushing the head of a sea monster or an octopus, representing Satan. Often, they are shown twisted around a trident or an anchor, suggesting Christ on the Cross. In underground Rome there is even an image of a dolphin with an exposed heart.

The dolphin usually symbolizes Jesus Christ. In some instances, however, the dolphin seems to represent not Christ, but Christians. Thus the dolphin, like the lamb, holds an ambiguous position for the ancients: the lamb can represent Christ as "Lamb of God" — or the Christian as member of the Good Shepherd's "little flock." These dolphin-Christians appear sometimes in pairs, both swimming toward a monogram or other symbol of Christ.

The dolphin appears more often than any other identifiable form of sea creature in early Christian art. It was commonly engraved on Christian rings. Very early in the fourth century, when the Emperor

Dolphins tied to the trident. *The Catacombs of St. Callistus, Rome. Third century.*

Constantine made the Lateran Basilica a gift to the Church, he illuminated its interior with many dolphin-shaped lamps made of gold and silver. The sixth-century **Book of the Popes** tells us that one chandelier, cast from "purest gold," weighed fifty pounds and included fifty dolphin-lamps. Another chandelier, made of silver, weighed fifty pounds and included twenty dolphins.

Ancient Sources:
- *Babylonian Talmud, **Bekoroth** 8a.*
- *Philo, **Alexander** 67.*

Modern Sources:
- *Charbonneau-Lassay, 306-308.*
- *Goodenough, 5:24, 27.*

A goblet with a dolphin (a fish?).
Detail from a mosaic from Domus dei pesci, Ostia, Italy. Third century.

Chapter 9
The Peacock

⁂

For the king had a fleet of ships of Tarshish at sea with the
fleet of Hiram. Once every three years the fleet . . . used to
come bringing gold, silver, ivory, apes, and peacocks.
1 Kings 10:22

Peacocks were, with gold and silver, unmistakable signs of King Solomon's wealth. With ivory and apes, they bespoke a luxury so great that it bordered on frivolity. Prized for their brilliant plumage, the birds brightened the courtyards of the estates of the wealthy.

For those inclined to meditation, the peacock was a lavish sign of God's artistry, and the divine Artist had fashioned the fowl to reveal a greater beauty, a divine beauty. Christians have always seen, in the eye-shaped pattern on the peacock's tail feathers, a symbol of the all-seeing eye of God.

Even when the peacock was molting, it was reflecting the life of God. For, as Christ suffered bodily death only to rise again in glory, so does the peacock lose its lovely feathers only to gain a more magnificent set. So will every faithful Christian gain a greater glory through the loss of the mortal body.

Thus, the peacock stood for resurrection, of Christ and of the Christian.

The bird's hard flesh led some of the ancients to speculate that it was incorruptible. St. Augustine — who was prone to see nature charged with signs of the supernatural — even performed a scientific experiment to see if the meat was subject to decay. He tells the curious story near the end of his book **City of God**:

Coptic stela with a peacock and a fish.
Luxor Museum, Egypt. Sixth century.

Peacock. *Vault painting from the Catacombs of Priscilla, Rome.*

The truth is that God . . . can give to the substance of flesh the qualities needed for existence in the world to come. After all, it was God the Creator of all things who gave the flesh of the peacock that property that keeps it from decaying even when dead. This property, when I first heard of it, seemed to me incredible. But it happened at Carthage that a bird of this kind was cooked and served to me. Taking a suitable slice of meat from its breast, I ordered it to be kept; and when it had been kept as many days as would cause any other meat to stink, it was brought out and set before me, and emitted no offensive smell. After it had been put away for thirty days and more, it was still in the same state. And a year later, it was still the same, except that it was a little more shriveled, and drier.

The peacock appears often at Christian gravesites, as a symbol of the most lavish gift the divine king could give. In the catacombs, the peacock adorns the walls near the loculi where the bodies of the dead lay exposed.

Unlike the meat of Augustine's peafowl, the bodies of Christians certainly gave way to molder and rot. And yet, after almost two millen-

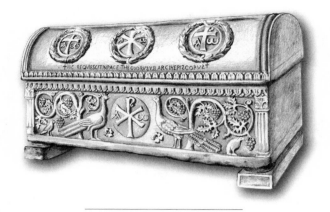

Sarcophagus of Bishop Theodorus.
Marble. St. Apollinare in Classe, Italy. End of fifth century.

nia, there stand the paintings of the peacocks, relatively incorrupt, where believers had placed them as enduring acts of faith, as visual creeds.

In the earliest baptismal creeds, the new Christians professed belief not just in "the resurrection of the body," but in "the resurrection of the flesh."

Ancient Sources:
- St. Hippolytus, **Apostolic Tradition** 21.17-18.
- St. Augustine, **City of God** 21.4.

Peacocks and vine. Detail from a border frieze from a floor mosaic in a house at Yakto, Turkey (now in Worcester Art Museum). Beginning of the fourth century.

Chapter 10
Milk

⌁

Like newborn babes, long for the pure spiritual milk, that by
it you may grow up to salvation.

1 Peter 2:2

Milk, in biblical religion, is always a sign of health, prosperity, and blessing. When God made His lavish promises to His chosen people, He spoke of the "blessings of the breasts" (Gen 49:25), and He led them to "a land flowing with milk and honey" (Ex 3:8). Nothing spoke so eloquently of earthly abundance as the milk of great herds of livestock. Nothing spoke so vividly of self-giving, life-giving love as the image of a mother nursing her child. The symbol finds its fullest and most poetic expression in the oracles of the Prophet Isaiah:

> "Rejoice with Jerusalem, and be glad for her,
>   all you who love her . . .
> that you may suck and be satisfied
>   with her consoling breasts;
> that you may drink deeply with delight
>   from the abundance of her glory."
> For thus says the Lord:
> "Behold, I will extend prosperity to her like a river,
>   and the wealth of the nations like an overflowing stream;
> and you shall suck, you shall be carried upon her hip,
>   and dandled upon her knees.
> As one whom his mother comforts,
>   so I will comfort you;
>   you shall be comforted in Jerusalem." (Is 66:10-13)

Maria Lactans — the oldest Egyptian representation of Our Lady. Coptic limestone grave stela from El Fayoum, Egypt (now in Staatliche Museen, Berlin). Fifth century.

God made all of creation to be a blessing to His faithful people. His people, in turn, discerned that creation's greatest blessings were signs of greater spiritual realities. The great Jewish commentator, Philo of Alexandria, a contemporary of Jesus, spoke of divine Wisdom as "the mother and nurse of the whole universe."

And the earliest Christian hymns continued to speak of milk, especially mother's milk, as a sign of God's grace, His spiritual gifts to humankind. In the so-called *Odes of Solomon*, from the late first or early second century, God compares Himself to a nursing mother:

> For I turn not my face from my own, because I know them.
> And before they had existed I recognized them . . .
> I fashioned their members, and my own breasts I prepared
>   for them,
> that they might drink my holy milk and live by it.

In another Ode, the human narrator speaks of the same gift from the human perspective:

Nursing figurine.
Pottery from Beth Shean, Israel. Israel Antiquities Authority. Fourth–fifth century.

One of the oldest Marian images.
Fresco from the Catacombs of Priscilla — Cubiculum of Velatio, Rome. Around A.D. 250.

> *And I was carried like a child by its mother;*
> *and He gave me milk, the dew of the Lord.*
> *And I was enriched by His favor, and rested in His*
> *perfection.*

God's grace in its fullness is a person: Jesus Christ; and St. Clement of Alexandria delights in speaking of Jesus as "milk" from the "care-soothing breast of God the Father." With the whole Christian tradition, Clement sees the baptismal font as the womb of the Church, from which believers receive second birth. Once born from Mother Church, God's children require feeding. Thus, for Clement, milk is an especially apt metaphor for Christ's real presence in the Eucharist. A Christian is "nourished with milk, the Lord's own nourishment as soon as we leave our mother's womb, and as soon as we are born anew. . . . Our nourishment, that is, the Lord Jesus, the Word of God, is Spirit become flesh, flesh from heaven made holy. This is our nourishment, the milk flowing from the Father by which alone we little ones are fed." Such images find further development in the fourth-century hymns of St. Ephrem of Syria. The fourth-century Syriac

Milk guarded by sheep.
Cemetery of St. Callistus, Rome. Second century.

Book of Steps succinctly made the connection between the Church's motherhood and its sacraments; it praised the visible Church, which "with its altar and baptism — gives birth to people as infants, who suckle milk until they are weaned."

The "milk-feeding" of newborn Christians had a quite literal expression in one beautiful and deeply symbolic ritual of the ancient Church — a rite that did not survive the age of the Fathers. In the liturgy of Easter Vigil, the newly baptized would proceed to receive their first Communion, under both species, both the bread and the chalice of wine. Immediately afterward, however, they were given a second chalice, this one filled with a mixture of milk and honey, and it signified their passage, through the sacraments, into the true promised land, the Kingdom of God, the Church of Jesus Christ. Tertullian witnesses to this rite in North Africa in the year A.D. 204, as does St. Hippolytus of Rome a few years later. The so-called **Epistle of Barnabas** testifies to the practice much earlier, perhaps at the end of the first century. St. Ambrose and St. Jerome both speak of the rite as commonplace at the end of the fourth century. The modern historian Cardinal Jean Danielou believed that the chalice of milk and honey was probably an inheritance from early Judaism. Indeed, it was customary for

Jews to give children a spoonful of honey when they received their first lessons on the Law of Moses, so that the law might always be sweet to them.

In Scripture and tradition, milk and honey were distinguishing signs of the promised land — the true home for God's chosen people. There, the herds and the flocks could thrive, under the care of the Good Shepherd. All these ideas come together in a single fourth-century Roman casket, whose decorations show Jesus as the Good Shepherd, milking a ewe, while its flanking panels show other scriptural images associated with baptism.

The ideas are equally vivid in the third-century **Passion of Saints Perpetua and Felicity**. While awaiting her martyrdom, young Perpetua — who is herself a nursing mother — has a series of ecstatic visions. In one, she sees a shepherd milking his sheep. He approaches Perpetua and pours milk into her cupped hands. As she drinks it, she hears the people around her say, "Amen!" It is clear from the narrative — which also depicts the singing of the "Holy, Holy, Holy" and the Sign of Peace — that the milk from this Good Shepherd is symbolic of the Eucharist. Immediately after receiving it, Perpetua awakes with a sweet taste in her mouth; and, at that moment, she receives the grace she needs in order to face her ultimate trial in the arena.

As the Mother of God, the Blessed Virgin Mary was a singular

Nursing figure.
Section of the mosaic floor from the church at Horvat Beer Shema, Western Negev, Israel.

channel of God's grace. It was she who brought the "milk of the Father" into the world. It should come as no surprise, then, that the earliest images of Mary depict her breastfeeding the child Jesus. This is true of the oldest Marian image in Rome, a third-century fresco in the Catacomb of Priscilla; it is true as well of the oldest Egyptian representation of Our Lady, a fifth-century Coptic engraving in limestone, at El Fayoum.

St. Ephrem sang of Jesus nursing at Mary's breast while He simultaneously nourished all the world, including His own mother!

> *He was lying there, sucking Mary's milk,*
> *Yet all created things suck from His goodness.*
> *He is the living breast; from His life*
> *The dead have sucked living breath — and come to life.*

The shepherd milking.
Fragment of a sarcophagus. Museo delle Terme, Rome. Third century.

As from their words, so from the images of our earliest Christian ancestors, we learn to live the life of grace, our life in Jesus Christ. At the end of the second century, St. Irenaeus of Lyons exhorted us to "take refuge in the Church, to drink milk at her breast, to be fed with the Scriptures of the Lord."

Babies can do very little to gain nourishment; they can only cry out in their need. So are we in our need of grace.

The Catholic Church is the "one and only mother," said St. Cyprian of Carthage. "By her bearing are we born, by her milk are we nourished."

Ancient Sources:

- *Philo of Alexandria,* **On Drunkenness** *31.*
- **Epistle of Barnabas** *6.*
- **Odes of Solomon** *8:12-14 and 35:5-6.*
- *St. Irenaeus of Lyons,* **Against Heresies** *5.20.2; see also 3.38.1.*
- **Passion of Perpetua and Felicity** *4 and 12.*
- *Tertullian,* **The Chaplet** *3.*
- *St. Clement of Alexandria,* **Christ the Teacher** *1.43-45.*
- *St. Hippolytus,* **The Apostolic Tradition** *23.*
- *St. Cyprian of Carthage,* **On the Unity of the Church** *4.*
- *St. Ephrem of Syria,* **Hymns on the Nativity** *4.149-150; see also* **Hymns on Paradise** *11.6;* **Hymns on the Church** *25.18;* **Hymns on the Resurrection** *1.7.*
- **The Book of Steps** *12.2.*
- *St. Jerome,* **Dialogue Against the Luciferians** *8.*
- *St. Ambrose of Milan,* **On the Sacraments** *5.17;* **Cain and Abel** *1.19.*

Modern Sources:

- *Danielou,* **Theology** *333-334.*
- *Goodenough, 6:118ff.*
- *Kaniyamparampil, 202-223.*
- *Musurillo,* **Symbolism** *49.*
- *Yarnold, 39.*
- *Plompe.*

Chapter 11
The Lamp

❧

You are my lamp, O Lord, and my God lightens my darkness.
2 Samuel 22:29

Lamps are unique in our discussion, because we must consider them as both a medium and a message — as a surface for presenting symbols and as a symbol themselves — and sometimes as both simultaneously.

The lamp is a common image in the Bible. The Psalmist uses it to symbolize God's word (Ps 119:105). Elsewhere, King David speaks of God Himself as a lamp (2 Sam 22:29). Proverbs invokes the lamp as a mataphor for the human spirit (Prv 20:27). In the Gospels, Jesus uses the lamp as a symbol of good works (Mt 5:15), of wisdom (Mt 25:1f), and of John the Baptist (Jn 5:35). For St. Peter, the lamp represents the prophetic word (2 Pt 1:19). In Revelation, the lamp is a sign of the current age, as distinct from the end of time, when "the Lord God will be their light" (Rev 22:5).

Yet even in the time of darkness — of testing and persecution — Jesus had promised to illumine the lives of the saints: "I am the light of the world; he who follows Me will not walk in darkness, but will have the light of life" (Jn. 8:12).

When the lamp appeared as an ornament in paintings, seals, and signets, it surely suggested all those biblical passages; for they would surely have been familiar as readings in the liturgy.

One of the earliest hymns we know, the Greek **Phos Hilaron**, is commonly called "Hymn for the Lighting of the Lamps," and the lyrics look to the lamps as a sign of Jesus Christ. St. Basil, writing in the fourth century, wrote: "It seemed fitting to our fathers not to receive the gift of the light at eventide in silence, but, on its appearing, immediately to give thanks [with] these words of thanksgiving at the lighting of the lamps."

Lamp with vine.

Lamp with a cross. Pottery from Beth Shean, Israel
(Collection of Christian Schmidt, Munich). Fourth century.

The hymn in use in his day St. Basil traces back to Athenogenes, a martyr from the beginning of the second century. Thus, from the earliest days of the Church, the faithful daily associated Christ with the lighted lamps.

It would surely serve as a powerful symbol, especially for Christians who lived in lands with minimal outdoor lighting. The major cities had flaming streetlamps, but the towns didn't, and the farmlands were hidden in blackness on a moonless night.

Think, too, of Christian worship in times of persecution. The earliest sources tell us that it took place before sunrise or after sunset, when an assembly might be less conspicuous. It took place behind closed doors, with the windows bolted shut. Thus, once again, when Christians knew Christ's real presence — in the Mass — they saw Him amid the lamplight.

In the generations immediately after the Church's peace, the Fathers witness to the continued use of lamps in the liturgy. It was not, moreover, merely a functional use. St. Jerome said, "Throughout all the churches of the east, whenever the Gospel is to be recited, they bring forth lights, even if it is noonday — not, certainly, to drive away darkness, but to manifest some sign of joy, that under the symbol of bodily light may be indicated that light of which we read in the Psalms: 'Your word is a lamp to my feet and a light to my paths.'" St. Gregory Nazianzen attests to the use of lamps in the baptismal liturgy, and many Fathers note their use in the ancient rites of Christian burial.

For St. Gregory, the brightness of the church's lamps was a symbol of the good works we take with us to judgment. They are also a symbol and foretaste of the perpetual light of heavenly glory. "The lamps that you will kindle," he said, "are a sacrament of the illumination there [in heaven] with which we shall meet the Bridegroom — we shining and virgin souls with the lamps of our faith shining."

The ancients fashioned lamps out of ceramics and metal, clay and bronze. In the eastern Mediterranean, they formed them in the shape of a slipper. Elsewhere, it was common to make them round. In the western lands, most people fueled their lamps with olive oil; the Persians, however, used the petroleum that bubbled up from the ground. In any case, oil lamps burned much brighter than wax candles, and they could be hung from chains, to project their light all the more.

The most popular pilgrimage destinations were the tombs of the apostles and martyrs. Some of these were aboveground in cemeteries; but many were underground, in dugout tunnels and abandoned mines — think of the catacombs — dark chambers with no natural sources of light. There, the lamps were necessary and plentiful. It was customary

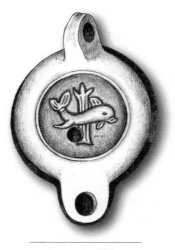

Lamp with a dolphin.

Lamp with wheat.

for pilgrims to carry small vials to collect oil from the lamps at the tombs of the saints. Christians revered these oils as relics and attributed healing power to them.

Potters made endless varieties of lamps, and many have survived to our day. They are the spent lightbulbs of the ancient world. While most are plain and homely, some have decorations — geometric motifs, words and phrases, and sometimes, family names. Occasionally the craftsmen signed the bottom of the lamp. As the Church grew, we find an increasing number of lamps decorated with Christian symbols: sheaves of wheat and clusters of grapes, the labarum, the fish, the boat, or a simple cross scratched into the clay. Again, these vary in quality; some are crudely drawn, and others are true works of art. Among the most interesting lamps are those that were molded entirely into symbolic shapes, such as a fish, a boat, or a dolphin. Almost immediately after the peace of the Church, the Emperor Constantine ordered hundreds of gold and silver lamps to be fashioned into chandeliers for Rome's Lateran Basilica, many of them cast in the form of dolphins. Afterward, dolphin-shaped lamps became quite fashionable items in church decoration.

Since many symbols were common to all the ancients, regardless of religion, it is often impossible to tell whether a lamp's decorations are Christian or pagan, devotional or merely decorative.

Sometimes, however, the truth emerges unmistakably, as if in the light of a thousand lamps. One of the most common phrases inscribed on these vessels is "Jesus Christ, the Light of the World." The medium is the message.

Ancient Sources:
- St. Basil, **On the Holy Spirit** 29.
- St. Jerome, **Against Vigilantius** 7.
- St. Gregory Nazianzen, **Oration** 40.46.

Modern Source:
- Goodenough/Neusner 59.

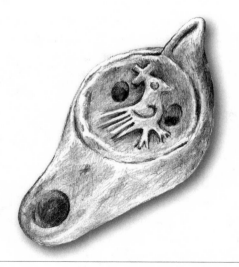

Lamp with a bird and a cross on its head. The Vatican Museum. Fourth century.

Chapter 12
Moses

⳹

They drank from the supernatural Rock which followed them,
and the Rock was Christ.
1 Corinthians 10:4

In the most common depiction of Moses in ancient Christian art, he isn't really Moses at all. He is a symbol of Peter, and that is made clear by annotation. The artists sometimes painted the Latin word "Petrus" above the head of the Moses figure. In several images, Peter appears receiving the divine law from Jesus Christ, just as Moses received the tablets of the law from God. Most often, however, Peter appears striking a rock with a stick, thereby releasing streams of water, just as Moses had done in the desert (Ex 17:6). There are well over a hundred incidences of this image in paleo-Christian art throughout the Roman world!

It is possible that the correspondence arose because of the similarity between the name Peter (*Petros*, *Petrus*) and the Greek and Latin words for "rock" (*Petra*). Hearing the Scriptures from First Corinthians or from Exodus, Christians could not help but make the association with the Prince of the Apostles.

When St. Paul discussed the incident in the desert (1 Cor 10:4), he spoke of it as a foreshadowing of baptism.

Thus, the pictures seem to say: As Moses released water for the refreshment of the Israelites, so Peter releases the waters of baptism for the redemption of all people. As Moses was a type of Jesus Christ, so he was also a type of Christ's vicar on earth, the Apostle Peter.

The images may also refer to an old tradition of Peter's final days on earth. Before his execution, so the story goes, he was incarcerated in the city prison near the Roman Forum, assigned to the dreaded Tullianum,

St. Peter as Moses striking the rock.
Glass. The Vatican Museum.

Peter's water miracle.
Detail from a sarcophagus. Museo delle Terme, Rome. Around A.D. 325.

the stinking subterranean cell. Not one to waste an opportunity, Peter preached the Gospel to his cellmates and jailers, eventually converting forty-seven men altogether. The jailers begged for baptism, but there was no water in the cell. Peter took up a stick and struck the rock floor, causing a pure spring to bubble up from below. Even today, if you visit the Mamertine Prison near the Roman Forum, you will see that a spring still flows from the floor.

We possess no written account of this incident earlier than late in the fourth century. It may be an oral tradition passed, like many others, from generation to generation of Roman Christians. It may also be an imaginative reading of the symbolic paintings of Moses as Peter.

Neither do we know for certain that Peter was imprisoned in the Tullianum. Some historians believe he was kept in house-arrest at a place not far from the Forum. We do know that the Church of Rome — in the fourth century and perhaps earlier — honored Peter's two jailers, Processus and Martinianus, as martyrs.

Peter-as-Moses images have been found most abundantly in and

Moses striking the rock.
The Catacombs of St. Callistus — Cubiculum of the Sheep, Rome. Fourth century.

St. Peter — Podgorica's cup. "Peter struck with his rod, and the founts began to run."—
PETRVS VIRGA PERQVODSET FONTIS CIPERVNT QVORERE.
From Podgorica (ancient Doclea), Montenegro. Fourth century.
The State Hermitage Museum, St. Petersburg.

around Rome — on sarcophagi, on gilded glass, and in murals — but not only in Rome. One was unearthed, for example, on a plate found in modern Montenegro. This last one bears the legend (in Latin): "Peter struck with his rod, and the founts began to run."

The Moses imagery recurs as well in the Fathers' discussions of the Prince of the Apostles. Aphrahat the Persian Sage makes the connection in the first half of the fourth century, as do Macarius of Egypt, Ephrem, Augustine, and Maximus of Turin after him. From Moses to Christ to Peter — Aphrahat makes complete the chain of associations, and he uses a dialect of the Aramaic language used by Jesus himself: "Moses brought forth water from the rock (kepha) for his people, and Jesus sent Simon Peter (Kepha) to carry his doctrine among the peoples."

The message of the images is clear. As God gave His authority on earth to Moses, and Moses in turn oversaw the life and worship of Israel, so the rites, the law, and the authority in the New Covenant pass from Jesus Christ to Peter, and from Peter to his successors, the popes.

Ancient Sources:

- *The Passion of the Apostle Peter According to the Bishop Linus* 5.
- *Aphrahat,* **Demonstrations** *21.10.*

Modern Sources:

- *Hertling and Kirschbaum, 195-196.*
- *Jensen,* **Understanding** *90-91, 121.*
- *Snyder, 101-102.*
- *Scaglia,* **Catacombs** *58-60.*
- *Allison, 106-109.*

Chapter 13
The Plow

⌒

They shall beat their swords into plowshares, and their spears
into pruning hooks; nation shall not lift up sword against
nation, neither shall they learn war any more.
Isaiah 2:4

For the early Christians, the plow was a reminder of Isaiah's prophecy of the gentle reign of the Messiah-King. Christ blessed the peacemakers
and refused to meet violence with violence. In agrarian societies, the plow
was an image of honest work and prosperity. A plow fashioned out of
weapons was a symbol of tranquility in order. The peaceful kingdom had
come, and Christians recognized it, even amid violent persecution.

Christ gave His people the means of making peace in the world.
St. Justin Martyr delighted in noting that Jesus, a carpenter by profession,
earned His living by making plowshares. Justin also noted that every plow
necessarily served as a crypto-cross — a reminder of the saving act that
brought about peace — since the structure of the tool required intersecting lines. "Without [the cross] there is no plowing."

Justin also invoked Isaiah's prophecy as he spoke of the peaceful
way Christians responded to their persecutors — not with revenge or
even violent self-defense, but with gentleness: "We who formerly used to
murder one another . . . now refrain from making war upon our enemies.
. . . We who, throughout the world, were filled with war and mutual
slaughter and every wickedness have changed our warlike weapons, our
swords, into ploughshares, and our spears into implements of tillage; and
we cultivate piety, righteousness, philanthropy, faith, and hope, which we
have from the Father himself through him who was crucified."

Around A.D. 190, St. Irenaeus developed the image of the plow into

Cain tills the soil.
The Miniatures of the Ashburnham Pentateuch (Bibliotheque Nationale, Paris).

an allegory of the incarnation. As a plow is made of wood and iron, so God brought peace on earth by the union of human and divine natures in Jesus Christ. Christ the maker of plows has Himself become the plow, which subdues the earth and brings peace. The new race of Christians, says Irenaeus, "are now unaccustomed to fighting. When struck, they turn the other cheek (Mt 5:39)." This was foretold by the prophets and is creditable to Jesus. "It is He Himself who has made the plough and introduced the pruning-hook . . . He has finally displayed the plow: the wood has been joined to the iron, and has thus cleansed his land, because the Word has been firmly united to flesh, affixed in its mechanism with nails, and has reclaimed the savage earth."

The saint had perhaps inherited this application of the image from an earlier generation. The apocryphal Acts of Peter, composed around A.D. 150, lists "plow" among the favored titles of Jesus. *The Infancy Gospel of Thomas* refers to Jesus and St. Joseph as makers of plows, undoubtedly to suggest the prophecy of Isaiah.

God emerges as a plowman — maybe — in the so-called "magical squares" that have been excavated from many ancient sites. Magical squares feature rows of letters whose sequence hides a secret meaning. The oldest known examples were discovered in the ruins of Pompeii, Italy. In that city, sealed by a volcanic eruption in A.D. 79, were two identical instances of a square made up of the Latin words: **Sator Arepo Tenet Opera Rotas**. If this puzzle indeed yields a Christian interpretation, as many scholars believe it does, then that would mean Christianity had spread to Pompeii at a very early date. It is certainly plausible, as "Sator Arepo" squares have turned up near the sites of other ancient Christian congregations. In Dura Europos, in Syria, archeologists found four of them, all identical to one another and to the squares in Pompeii.

The plow. Ossuary —
Dominus Flevit ("The Lord Wept") Church on the Mount of Olives, Israel.

Here is the square.

$$SATOR$$
$$AREPO$$
$$TENET$$
$$OPERA$$
$$ROTAS$$

It presents palindromes in every direction. And if it is a sentence, a rough translation might be: "The sower in his field controls the workings of his tools." If we read it as a Christian allegory, the sower would represent God, and his "field" the earth. His tools are his faithful people, who do his will.

Read as anagrams, the lines can yield a horizontal and a vertical *Pater Noster* (Latin for "Our Father"). The two intersecting *Pater Nosters*, then, would form a Greek cross, with each beam capped by an A and an Ω, *alpha* and *omega*.

It is all speculation; but it has the weight of some mighty authorities behind it. The great scholar of early Christianity, Cardinal Jean Daniélou, argued persuasively that St. Irenaeus was familiar with the Sator Arepo square and referred to it in his teaching, especially in his references to the plow.

But as far back as the fourth century, St. Gregory of Elvira put it all in a far less puzzling way when he wrote that Jesus "is called the plow because our stony hearts are subjected to the sign of his cross to be prepared for the seeds they need."

Ancient Sources:

- St. Justin Martyr, **Dialogue** 88, 110; **First Apology** 39, 55.
- St. Irenaeus of Lyons, **Against the Heresies** 4.34.4.
- **Acts of Peter** 20.
- **Infancy Gospel of Thomas** 13.1.
- St. Gregory of Elvira, **On the Orthodox Faith** 6.

Modern Source:

- Daniélou, **Primitive** 89-101.

Chapter 14
Vessels

꙳

But we have this treasure in earthen vessels, to show that the
transcendent power belongs to God and not to us.
2 Corinthians 4:7

The sites of early Christian worship and burial yield shards of many different kinds of ceramic and glass vessels: decanters, bowls, vases, chalices. The same vessels are depicted in Christian paintings, sculpture, medals, and coins. We do not know whether the artists intended these objects to be symbolic or merely decorative.

Any vessel, however, is suggestive of what it might contain. In a Christian context, that might be water for baptism, wine for the Eucharist, or oil for anointing. There are stories, too, of Christian women who ventured out to soak up the blood of martyrs and collect it in vessels for burial.

Some artists painted ceramic bowls overfull with fruit, like horns of plenty. These might indicate the abundance of God's creation or the lavishness of the heavenly banquet. The latter interpretation seems appropriate for the art of the catacombs. These frescoes might also be merely still-life paintings, meaning no more than what they depict.

Both Tertullian and Eusebius tell us that the ancient churches kept vessels of water for worshippers to cleanse themselves on entering. Describing a newly built church in Tyre, Eusebius notes that at the entrances were fonts, "symbols of sacred purifications . . . which furnish an abundance of water with which those who come within the sanctuary may purify themselves. This is the first halting-place of those who enter." Both men assume that the washing was symbolic rather than practical. It was a sign of the forgiveness of sins. It is possible that some of the catacomb

Pilgrim flask of St. Menas.
Clay. Louvre, Paris. Fourth–sixth century.

Ampulla with a cross and two birds. Pottery. Eastern Mediterranean.
Collection of Christian Schmidt, Munich. Sixth century.

art represents these vessels. It is possible, too, that the blessing of water in the fourth-century Liturgy of St. Serapion is for this purpose — the holy-water fonts that Catholics, then as now, built into the entrances of their churches.

Zoomorphic vessel with a cross.
Pottery. Provenance unknown.
Collection of Christian Schmidt, Munich. Fifth–sixth century.

The Attarouthi treasure.
Silver and sliver with gilding. From Attarouthi, Syria
(now at the Metropolitan Museum of Art). A.D. 500–650.

Ancient Sources:

- Tertullian, **On Prayer** 13.
- Eusebius, **Church History** 10.4.40.

The Vrap treasure. Silver and gold.
Found in Vrap, Albania (now at the Metropolitan Museum of Art).

Chapter 15
The Lamb

༱

The Lamb will conquer them, for He is Lord of lords
and King of kings, and those with Him are called
and chosen and faithful.
Revelation 17:14

In the art of Christian antiquity, the lamb appears most often in the arms of the Good Shepherd. There, the lamb represents the believer, safe in the care of Jesus Christ. Jesus Himself hallowed this use of the image when he told Simon Peter: "Feed my lambs" (Jn 21:15).

When the lamb appears alone, however, it usually signifies Christ Himself. He is the "Lamb of God," hailed as such by John the Baptist (Jn 1:29 and 36). He is "the Lamb" enthroned victorious, whom the Book of Revelation mentions twenty-eight times, and whose "marriage supper" marks the end of the Bible and the culmination of history (Rev 19:9).

The New Testament, in fact, repeatedly identifies Jesus with this curious symbol: a sheep in its infancy. To most non-Jewish observers, it would seem a baffling symbol of divinity.

But to Jews the lamb represented the sacrifice that sealed and renewed God's covenant with His people Israel. It signified the great saving event of their history: the exodus from slavery in Egypt. The Book of Exodus (chapter 12) tells how God prepared Israel before He sent His tenth and final plague upon the obstinate Egyptians. He instructs each family to sacrifice a lamb and paint the doorpost of their dwelling with its blood. If they did so, the angel of death would "pass over" their homes when coming to slay the firstborn son in every household.

Ever after, the people marked that day with the great feast of Pesach, the Passover. It was a celebration of the birthday of their nation, their

The Good Shepherd.
Marble. The Vatican Museum. Around A.D. 300.

The Sacrifice of Isaac.
Detail from the Mas d'Aire Sarcophagus. Aire-sur-l'Adour, France. Around A.D. 270.

liberation by the hand of God through the ritual sacrifice of the lamb. The "saving" lamb would reappear, some centuries later, in an oracle of the Prophet Isaiah, who compares a suffering servant of God to a lamb. "He was oppressed, and he was afflicted, yet he opened not his mouth; like a lamb that is led to the slaughter, and like a sheep that before its shearers is dumb, so he opened not his mouth" (Is 53:7; see also Jer 11:19). The lamb's suffering, however, once again would bring about the salvation of God's people: "He was wounded for our transgressions, he was bruised for our iniquities; upon him was the chastisement that made us whole, and with his stripes we are healed" (Is 53:5).

For these passages and others, Christians would come to call the Book of Isaiah the "fifth Gospel," because it anticipated many of the main themes and events of Jesus' ministry. For Christians, Jesus was that suffering servant, slaughtered like a lamb for the life of the people.

There is a recurrent Passover theme throughout the New Testament. Matthew tells us that Jesus foretold His impending death in "paschal" terms: "The Passover is coming, and the Son of man will be delivered up to be crucified" (Mt 26:2). John's narrative turns upon the three Passover celebrations in the last three years of Jesus' life. John informs us that Jesus died upon the cross at precisely the hour the priests were sacrificing the lambs in the Temple (Jn 19:14).

The Acts of the Apostles makes an explicit connection between Isaiah's suffering servant and Jesus Christ (Acts 8:32). St. Paul, too, identifies Jesus with the Passover victim: "Christ, our paschal lamb, has been sacrificed" (1 Cor 5:7), as does St. Peter, who speaks of "the precious blood of Christ, like that of a lamb without blemish or spot" (1 Pt 1:19).

In Christian art and preaching, then, the lamb appears paradoxical: bloody, but victorious; slaughtered, but life-giving; meek, yet all-powerful. John the Seer describes his vision of the glorious Christ in heaven as that of "a Lamb standing, as though it had been slain" (Rev 5:6).

As the lamb was the sign of the Old Covenant with the Jews, Christ Himself was the sign and the sacrifice of the new Passover. As God

Lamb of God on sarcophagus.
St. Apollinare in Classe, Italy.

required the Israelites to consume the paschal lamb, so Jesus commanded the people of the New Covenant to "eat the flesh of the Son of man and drink his blood" (Jn 6:53).

As Passover had been the central feast for the Jews, it remained the central feast for Christians. The English term "Easter" obscures this fact. In most languages, the feast of the Resurrection is called by the same name as the Passover: Pesach, Pascha, Pasqua, Pasch. This close connection was so important to the early Christians that it became the subject of their most intense and divisive controversies — the question of when and how to mark the Passover. Many in the eastern churches celebrated on the

St. Agnes with a lamb.
Mosaic from St. Apollinare Nuovo, Ravenna. A.D. 557–570.

Lamb of God.
Vault mosaic in the sanctuary of St. Vitale, Ravenna. A.D. 547.

very day of the Jewish Passover, while Christians in the west thought the observance belonged on a Sunday.

All the Church, however, agreed that Christ was the Lamb of the new and everlasting Passover, and that the Lamb was consumed in the Eucharist. The image of the lamb suggested the salvation, the sacrifice, and the sacrament. Over time, the Eucharistic liturgy accumulated prayers that speak of Jesus as the lamb: the **Gloria**, a most ancient hymn that addresses Christ as "Lord God, Lamb of God," and, of course, the **Agnus Dei**, which literally means "Lamb of God."

In the so-called "paschal homily" of St. Melito of Sardis we may possess the heart of an early Easter liturgy, in which the preacher makes clear the continuity between the old Passover and the new, the old lamb and the new.

> *The law is old, but the gospel is new.*
> *The type was temporary, but grace is forever.*

The sheep was corruptible, but the Lord is incorruptible.
He was crushed as a lamb, but resurrected as God.
He was led to sacrifice as a sheep, yet he was not a sheep.
And though he was like a lamb without voice, yet he was
    not a lamb.
The one was the model; the other was the finished product.
For God took the place of the lamb,
and a man took the place of the sheep.
But in the man was Christ, who contains all things.

Catacomb art sometimes depicts a lamb beside a crypto-cross, such as an anchor. St. Paulinus of Nola described a fourth-century church in Italy, where "Under the bloody cross is Christ as a snowy white lamb."

In later art, the Lamb of God was sometimes given an exalted appearance, with a halo around its head and other symbols of divinity. This might have lent itself to misunderstanding by non-Christians — and even accusations of idolatry. In 692, the so-called "Council in Trullo" actually issued legislation temporarily forbidding artwork that portrayed Christ as a lamb! The gathering was much concerned with liturgical abuses and misunderstandings, and the assembled bishops directed that artwork should be realistic rather than symbolic — a clear break with the sen-

Lamb with a caduceus.
Fresco from the Catacombs of Vigna Randanini, Rome.

sibilities of the earliest Christian generations. The western church never recognized that gathering as an ecumenical council; nor were its canons considered binding in the west.

The ancient Christians sometimes used the lamb to symbolize other people or virtues. Melito refers to the Blessed Virgin Mary as a "ewe lamb." The Roman child-martyr St. Agnes is often depicted as a lamb or holding a lamb — because of her youth and innocence, and because her name literally means "lamb." To St. Clement of Alexandria, all Christian women were "beautiful ewe lambs."

Ancient Sources:

[a]   *St. Melito of Sardis,* **On Passover** *4-5.*

[a]   *St. Paulinus of Nola,* **Letters** *32.*

[a]   *Clement,* **Exhortation** *12.*

[a]   *Council in Trullo, canon 82.*

Modern Source:

[a]   *Hahn,* **Lamb's Supper** *14-27.*

Chapter 16
The Dove

❧

O that I had wings like a dove!
I would fly away and be at rest.
Psalm 55:6

For Christians of a later age, the figure of a dove in sacred art almost always signifies the person of the Holy Spirit. This is the case only in a limited number of works of ancient Christian art, most of them narrative scenes that depict the baptism of Jesus in the River Jordan. In these scenes, as in the Gospel (Mt 3:16), the Holy Spirit descends upon Jesus "like a dove" or "in the form of a dove."

Among the ancients, however, the dove almost always represented the soul of the believer. (We find this in Greek literature as far back as Plato's **Phaedrus**, and in Egyptian inscriptions reaching back to the age of the Pharaohs.) In funerary art especially, it depicts the soul of the departed. Sometimes in Christian art, for example, the dove will appear beside an orant figure, accompanied by a proper name and occasionally by words that make the symbolic connection very clear: "Most innocent soul" or "Soul without guile." The dove holding an olive branch, harking back to the dove sent out by Noah to find dry land (Gen 8:8-11), signifies a soul at rest, having found what it wanted and needed. The olive branch was, among the ancients, a universal symbol of peace.

Some images symbolically depict the dove as a soul refreshing itself with the sacraments, dipping into a font of water (baptism) or pecking at grapes or grain (the Eucharist).

We find a beautiful literary example of the soul symbolized by a dove in the second-century account of the Martyrdom of Polycarp. When the flames fail to kill the elderly bishop, an executioner comes forward "to

Funerary mosaic with an orant and doves.
From Tabarka, Tunis (now in the Bardo Museum). Fourth century.

Orant with two doves. Grave stone, Rome. The Vatican Museum.

pierce him through with a dagger." When this was done, "a dove came forth" from the wound. St. Polycarp had died, and his soul had separated from his body.

The spiritual soul, through the ministry of the Church — and, ultimately, through a holy death — finds its way home to God, who is Spirit (Jn 4:24). Said St. Clement of Alexandria: "It is not without singular grace that the soul is winged and rises on high, laying aside all weight and giving itself over to what is akin to it."

In the Middle Ages, it was common to reserve the Eucharist in a dove-shaped receptacle suspended from the church's ceiling. Some scholars believe that the custom goes back to the early Church. An early biography of St. Basil reports that he had such a dove cast in pure gold, and inside the dove he would place a portion of the sacrament. The early existence of such Eucharistic doves would help to explain some cryptic lines in the writings of other Fathers. Tertullian, for example, says in one place: "The house of our dove is simple; it is found on elevated sites, is always open, and is placed toward the light. For the image of the Holy Spirit loves the direction of the rising sun, which is the symbol of Christ." St. John Chrysostom speaks of the sacrament as "laid on the altar, not wrapped in swaddling clothes, but vested with the Holy Ghost," another possible reference to the Eucharistic dove. Later histories report that the Emperor Constantine presented Pope St. Sylvester I with a golden dove for reservation of the Eucharist in St. Peter's Basilica. In the fifth century,

Victoria epitaph dedicated to a consecrated virgin. The Vatican Museum. Fourth century.

Sedulius wrote: "And the Holy Spirit in the form of a dove has robed Christ in honor." Taken together, these dove quotes are quite suggestive, though none is explicit enough to give us certainty.

Ancient Sources:
- Plato, **Phaedrus.**
- **Martyrdom of Polycarp** 16.
- St. Clement of Alexandria, **Tapestries** 5.83.1-2.
- Tertullian, **Against the Valentinians** 3.
- St. John Chrysostom, **To the People of Antioch, Homily** 13.
- Sedulius, **Letter 12.**

Modern Sources:
- Marucchi, 282-284.
- Murphy, 72.

Dove holding a crown.
Graffito from the Catacombs of St.
Callistus, Rome. Third century.

Dove pecking grapes.
Grafitto from the Catacombs of St.
Callistus, Rome. Third century.

Chapter 17
Bread and Sheaves

❧

Unless a grain of wheat falls into the earth and dies, it
remains alone; but if it dies, it bears much fruit.
John 12:24

Bread appears frequently in early Christian art, and sheaves of wheat are a common decorative motif. The bread usually appears as round loaves or wafers; since many of the images have a two-dimensional quality, it is impossible to tell whether it is leavened or flat bread. Sometimes the loaves overlie a single fish or several fish. The two elements together symbolize the real presence of the mystic fish (ICHTHYS in Greek, see chapter 1), Jesus Christ, in the eucharistic bread. They also suggest the Gospel stories of Jesus multiplying loaves and fishes (e.g., Mt 14:19 and 15:36). Those stories come to mind, again, when we see another common early Christian image: that of bread piled high in wicker baskets; the evangelists report that after Jesus fed the multitudes, the leftover portions filled many baskets. Indeed, St. Jerome tells us that churches constrained by poverty would serve the Eucharist in wicker baskets. Other sources, however, record that even poor churches strove to provide precious vessels for the Mass. And Jerome himself elsewhere said that priests should be taught to venerate the sacred vessels.

Sometimes the bread we see in paintings and inscriptions bears the sign of the cross, or a cross superimposed upon the letter X (*chi*), the initial of the Greek word for Christ. It was common for commercial bakers to mark their bread with a distinctive stamp. It was common for later Christians to mark their eucharistic bread with Christian symbols or words, as the churches still do today. It is likely that the earliest Christians, too, gave their bread some distinguishing mark.

*Miracle scene. Detail from the Sarcophagus of Marcus Claudianus
(now in the Museo delle Terme, Rome). A.D. 330–335.*

The Food of Life.
Lid of a sarcophagus (Museo delle Terme, Rome). Third century.

Sheaves of wheat are also very common decorations, in Christian contexts as in Jewish and pagan. They often line the seams of lamps and other ceramic objects. They decorate the borders of tombs and the reverse sides of coins. It is impossible, though, to determine whether these are symbolic or merely decorative. Sometimes, too, it is difficult to determine whether the crude etchings depict sheaves of grain or palm branches.

For a Christian, the wheat and the bread could only refer to Jesus, who called Himself the Bread of Life (Jn 6), who broke bread and called it His body (Mk 14:22), and who compared His death to the germination of a grain of wheat (Jn 12:24). He promised that the grain of wheat, dying, would bear "much fruit" — and the fruit of the grain is surely bread, as for Jews the "fruit of the vine" is wine.

The Fathers and the Scriptures abundantly attest to the centrality of the Eucharist — "the breaking of the bread" (Acts 2:42) — in the life of the Church. One can easily fill a book just with the testimonies from the first three centuries.

From gathered wheat to consecrated bread, the image is nowhere

Miracle of loaves and fishes. Sacristy of the Cathedral, Salerno, Italy.

Coptic oil lamp. Clay. From Oxyrhynchus, Egypt (now in the Petrie Museum of Egyptian Archeology, London). Coptic.

better summarized than in the earliest eucharistic prayer that has survived, that of the **Didache**, from the mid-first century: "And concerning the broken bread [pray this way]: "We thank You, our Father, for the life and knowledge which You made known to us through Jesus Your servant; to You be the glory forever. Even as this broken bread was scattered over the hills, and was gathered together and became one, so let Your Church be gathered together from the ends of the earth into Your kingdom; for Yours is the glory and the power through Jesus Christ for ever."

Orant with a bread basket and doves.
Incised slab of the deceased Criste from the Catacombs of Domitilla, Rome.

Inscription of Bincentia flanked by a Christogram and a basket filled with bread.
Loculus from the Catacombs of St. Sebastian, Rome.

Ancient Sources:

- *St. Jerome,* **Letter** *125.20;* **Letter** *114.2.*
- *Didache 9.*

Modern Source:

- *Aquilina,* **The Mass of the Early Christians.**

Chapter 18
The Crown

✧

Be faithful unto death, and I will give you the crown of life.
Revelation 2:10

The crown was, in the ancient world, a sign of privileged social standing — of public office, hereditary nobility, cultic priesthood, or military rank. It could also serve as a sign of temporary, festive status. Winning athletes were crowned for their achievements.

A bride and groom were "king" and "queen" for a day, at least at their own celebration, and so they might wear crowns as a sign of their special dignity. When victorious armies marched home in triumph, every soldier wore a palm crown.

Pagan Romans customarily crowned their beloved dead during funeral rites. This was the "crowning moment" of a life fully lived. Some considered the crown to signify a share in the life of a god. On the emperor, the crown represented his supposed divinity. On the dead, it was a sign of their elevated status in the afterlife.

A Jewish text of the second century B.C., the **Book of Jubilees**, tells us that Jews wore crowns when they celebrated the annual feast of Tabernacles. The Roman historian Tacitus reports that Jewish priests wore crowns of ivy.

Some rare ancient crowns were like their modern counterparts — precious metal studded with jewels. Most, however, were wreaths or garlands wound from flowers, laurel branches, or palms leaves.

The Book of Revelation tells of the martyrs wearing crowns in heaven. The second-century visionary Hermas also reports that faithful Christians, after death and judgment, received palm crowns from the

St. Peter and St. Paul.
Gold glass. The Vatican Museum. Fourth century.

angels. Similar imagery recurs in the first-century Jewish-Christian **Odes of Solomon**.

St. Clement of Alexandria held that faithful Christians, even on earth, wore Christ Himself as their jeweled crown. He interpreted the baptismal rite of anointing as a sort of coronation. "The anointed ones wear Christ symbolically on the head. They are unconsciously adorned with the head of the Lord. The precious stone, or pearl, or emerald, points out the Word Himself. The gold, again, is the incorruptible Word, who admits not the poison of corruption. The Magi, accordingly, brought to Him on His birth, gold, the symbol of royalty. And this crown, after the image of the Lord, fades not as a flower."

In the same generation, Minucius Felix contrasted Christian "crowns" with those of the pagans. For this magistrate, too, the Christian's crown was the permanent mark bestowed by baptism. "Pardon us if we do not crown our heads . . . Nor do we crown the dead . . . We do not bind ourselves to a withering garland, but we wear one living with eternal flowers from God."

Labarum in a crown. Fragment of a sarcophagus. The Vatican Museum. Late fourth century.

The Chrismon Cross crowned by the hand of God in the starry sphere.
Dome mosaic from the baptistery of San Giovanni in Fonte, Naples, Italy. Around A.D. 400.

His contemporary and fellow jurist Tertullian, however, took a much harder line, and issued a blistering attack on the pagan custom of wearing crowns. It is the subject of an entire essay by the North African controversialist: **De Corona Militum** — literally, "On the Military Crowns," but usually translated as "The Chaplet."

Tertullian begins his essay by conveying a piece of fresh news: A Christian soldier, handed a crown upon a victory in battle, quietly declined to wear it. The man was soon imprisoned for his impertinence. In prison at the time of Tertullian's composition, he would soon be "crowned more worthily with the white crown of martyrdom."

Tertullian goes on to take several lines of argument against the wearing of crowns: first, it is unnatural, as flowers belong in fields, and not woven into garlands; next, it is a custom that the pagans trace back to mythological gods, whom the Christians know to be demons; and lastly, only God should be crowned. Tertullian concludes by charging that any Christian who wears such festive crowns is guilty of idolatry and apostasy, since the army's victory ceremonies were invariably accompanied by pagan rites and sacrifices. "Even if the Christian says nothing with his mouth, he makes his response by having the crown on his head."

Tertullian's rage notwithstanding, the crown, the wreath, and the garland were, from the beginning, popular Christian symbols. They represent the Christian's participation in divine life through baptism — God's "crowning" of our human nature with a share of His own divine nature (see 2 Pt 1:4). The crown also signifies the Christian's victory over death, when Christ comes to the faithful departed, "to give them a garland instead of ashes" (Is 61:3).

In art and in religious literature, the early Christians associated the crown most especially with martyrdom. The symbol undoubtedly connects the martyrs' suffering with that of Jesus Christ, who was crowned with thorns; but the crown also evokes the victory portrayed in the Book of Revelation.

The poet Prudentius titled his anthology of historical poems *The Martyrs' Crowns.*

An equivalent image to the crown is the palm branch held in the hand (see Rev 7:9).

Marble chancel screen decorated in relief with a cross-flower within a wreath flanked by crosses. From Massuot Yizhad, Northern Negev, Israel. Sixth century.

St. Paul holding a crown and a scroll.
Sarcophagus fragment. The Vatican Museum.

Ancient Sources:
- *Jubilees* 16.30.
- Tacitus, *Histories* 5.5.
- Hermas, *Similitudes* 8.2.1.
- *Odes of Solomon* 1.1; 20.7-8.
- St. Clement of Alexandria, *The Teacher* 2.8.
- Minucius Felix, *Octavius* 38.
- Prudentius, *The Martyrs' Crowns*.

Modern Source:
- Danielou, *Primitive* 1-24.

Chapter 19
The Banquet

ℱ

He brought me to the banqueting house,
and his banner over me was love.
Song of Songs 2:4

The most arresting image from the early Church is perhaps the most enigmatic. It is the image that admits of the most divergent interpretations, and the one that most challenges us to adopt the mindset of the first Christians. It is the banquet.

The scene appears fairly often in murals, and with some common features. A number of people (usually seven) sit at a C-shaped table, with a meal of fish and bread before them. Sometimes there is wine on the table as well. Most of the diners are male, though there is sometimes a lone woman.

The question remains: What sort of meal do these paintings depict? The proposed answers — and they are many — tend to fall into two categories: those that view the scene as realistic, and those that see it as symbolic.

The "realistic" interpreters hold that the scene is more or less a mirror of the normal activity of the Christian congregation. The earliest Christian writers speak often of certain meals the Church held regularly. Even pagan authors — most famously, Pliny the Younger and the playwright Fronto — identified the common meal as the most characteristic Christian activity. What were these meals? We know of at least three distinct types of meal practiced during the first generations of Christianity.

1. The Eucharist. St. Justin Martyr commented that by his day, circa 150, "There is not one single race of men . . . among whom prayers and Eucharist are not offered through the name of the

The Banquet.
Fragment from the Sarcophagus of Hertofile, Rome.

crucified Jesus." The Eucharist always included bread and wine, though other elements may have been permitted in different times and places (the cup of milk and honey, for example). In the first generation, it is possible that the Eucharist was customarily celebrated in conjunction with a fuller, formal meal, known as:

2. The *Agape*, or "love feast." The New Testament (see Jude 12), the Didache, St. Ignatius of Antioch, and many other early sources attest to these full banquets of the Christian community. It seems, however, that from the beginning there were problems in associating the Eucharist with these feasts (see 1 Cor 11), and by the turn of the first century the Church had begun to separate the simpler Eucharist from the more elaborate Agape.

3. The Refrigerium. It was common for the ancients to celebrate funeral banquets after the burial rites of their beloved. Christians

Seven loaves and two fishes.
Mosaic from St. Apollinare Nuovo, Ravenna. Before A.D. 529.

Agape meal.

Fresco from the Catacombs of Sts. Peter and Marcellinus, Rome. Fourth century.

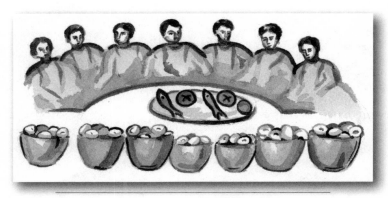

The meal of the seven with loaves and fishes and the seven baskets.
Fresco from the Catacombs of St. Callistus. After A.D. 200.

held to this custom; and some also remembered the departed with a meal, sometimes at the graveside, on the yearly anniversary of their passing. These memorial meals, called Refrigeria, are the origin of the Christian custom of celebrating saints' "feast days."

It is conceivable that any or all of these ritual meals could have taken place in the rooms where we find banquet paintings. The agape is probably the least likely candidate for a realistic reading. The custom seems to have faded by the middle of the third century; perhaps it had become unwieldy as Church membership grew.

Some historians note that Jews of the first through third centuries observed a Friday-evening meal that Tertullian called the *cena pura*. They believe that Jewish-Christians continued this observance, and that the Christian *cena pura* is what we glimpse on the walls of the catacombs. This hypothesis, however, requires several speculative leaps, and has not won much acceptance.

Another realistic — or at least narrative — candidate as model for the banquet scene is the Last Supper of Jesus Christ. This, however, is unlikely, as few of the murals portray thirteen diners at the table; and, often enough, at least one of those seated is female.

The symbolic reading demands no such rigor, especially for those who say the scene stands simply for an abstract concept like "fellowship" or "abundance," or "charity."

Some say, however, it is a symbolic portrayal of the "eschatological banquet" — the heavenly or messianic feast — evoked in both testaments of the Bible, as well as in the Jewish and Christian apocalyptic literature.

Consider the oracle of Isaiah: "On this mountain the Lord of hosts will make for all peoples a feast of fat things, a feast of wine on the lees, of fat things full of marrow, of wine on the lees well refined" (Is 25:6).

Consider, too, the allegory of the Book of Proverbs: "Wisdom has built her house . . . She has slaughtered her beasts, she has mixed her wine, she has also set her table. She has sent out her maids to call . . . 'Come, eat of my bread and drink of the wine I have mixed'" (Prv 9:1-6).

In the Gospel of Luke, Jesus tells a parable that compares the Kingdom of God to a banquet: "A man once gave a great banquet, and invited many; and at the time for the banquet he sent his servant to say to those who had been invited, 'Come; for all is now ready'" (Lk 14:16-17).

Funerary banquet.
Fresco from the Catacombs of Sts. Peter and Marcellinus, Rome.

And the Bible ends, of course, with the end of history, which John the Seer describes as the "marriage supper of the Lamb" (Rev 19:9).

All of these biblical details have been applied to the catacomb paintings by partisan interpreters.

It is possible, however, that most of the interpreters, both the symbolists and the realists, possess a bit of the truth. A eucharistic interpretation permits us to see each scene as both representational and symbolic, both scriptural and contemporary. First: The banquet paintings certainly evoke small details of real-life scenes that were familiar to Christian congregations. Second: The artworks just as surely allude to biblical scenes: by showing a meal of bread and fish, for example, they suggest the multiplication of loaves; and by showing bread and wine, the Last Supper. Third: These biblical scenes — as well as the others mentioned earlier — are commonly given a eucharistic interpretation by the early Fathers. This, too, was the intended effect of the ancient artists. Fourth: The abstract candidates for a purely symbolic reading are concepts the Fathers and the Scriptures associate with the Eucharist — the Greek word for fellowship (*koinonia*) can also be translated as "communion," with all of that word's modern resonances (see Acts 2:42). Fifth and finally: The early Fathers unanimously viewed the Eucharist itself as the heavenly banquet, Christ's parousia, His coming into their midst.

Why, then, are there usually seven diners? Some interpreters say that the number is meant to suggest the bread-and-fish meal at the end of John's Gospel, where we find Jesus eating with seven of His disciples. We know, too, that seven is the biblical number associated with the covenant; and the Eucharist is the "New Covenant" meal par excellence (Lk 22:20).

Why is there a lone woman in some banquet scenes? The lone woman, usually in the orant posture (see chapter 2), represents the Church, which is always portrayed as feminine: bride to the bridegroom Christ.

And what is the meaning of the fish at a Eucharistic gathering? It represents the presence of Christ, whom so many of the Fathers called the mystic fish (see chapter 1).

Early Christian art rarely presents anything in a merely realistic manner. It is beyond symbolic. It is symbolist — or, better, sacramental. It depicts common material things and ordinary events as signs of deeper spiritual realities. Even when an artist presents an historic or everyday scene, he is probably engaging the viewer's mind as well, giving "more than meets the eye."

If the banquet scenes are not mirrors of the ancient Eucharist, they are profoundly eucharistic in their message.

Ancient Sources:

- *Pliny the Younger,* **Letters** *10.96-97.*
- *Marcus Cornelius Fronto, fragment quoted in Minucius Felix,* **Octavius** *9.*
- *St. Justin Martyr,* **Dialogue** *41.*
- *Tertullian,* **To the Nations** *1.13.*

Chapter 20
The Lighthouse

⌁

Behold, I will . . . raise my signal to the peoples.
Isaiah 49:22

The lighthouse stands as a symbol of the Christian faith. The second-century Roman layman Hermas describes a vision he was granted — of the building of a stone tower near the waterside. And he explains it as an allegory of the Church: built by the waters of baptism, reaching up to heaven, constructed by angels, who fit together the "stones" that are the apostles, bishops, martyrs, confessors, and saints.

Hermas's tower was symbolic. But it was not unusual to find real towers by the seaside. Lighthouses raised their beacons at the entrances to many major harbors. And the greatest of all was the lighthouse in the harbor of Alexandria, Egypt. Named after the small island it occupied, the skyscraping Pharos was one of the seven wonders of the ancient world. Completed in 283 B.C., it was 440 feet tall, much taller than the Statue of Liberty. Like the presence of God in the Book of Exodus, the Pharos was engulfed in an enormous cloud by day and a bright fire by night. Its fame was such that its name became the generic term for a lighthouse. Sailors would speak of "the pharos of Carthage" or the "pharos at Ostia." Indeed, many distant lighthouses were modeled after the great one at Alexandria, with its three-tiered structure.

Alexandria was a major hub for trade and travel, so many Christians who worked at sea saw the Pharos for themselves — and never forgot the sight. Traveling apostles and missionaries would have known it well. St. Mark the Evangelist was said to be the city's first bishop; and in medieval images he is often portrayed with the Pharos as backdrop.

St. Mark's successors would inherit this luminous association.

The harbor of Portus.
Sarcophagus fragment from the Isola Sacra necropolis, Ostia, Italy (now in Museo Ostiense).

Funerary inscription.
The Giordani Catacombs, Rome. The Vatican Museum. Third century.

Around A.D. 371, St. Basil of Caesarea wrote a warm tribute to St. Athanasius, the Patriarch of Alexandria, who was then a very old man. Basil compares Alexandria's brilliant bishop to the great beacon in its harbor: "You see everything in all directions in your mind's eye like a man looking from some tall watchtower, while at sea many ships sailing together are all dashed one against the other by the violence of the waves." Over all the turmoil in the Church and the world, Athanasius — like the Church and the faith he served — could stand as a judge and a guide.

The simile readily came to mind for travelers in Egypt and pilgrims to its desert shrines. St. John Cassian used the Pharos in his description of Abbot Piamun, who governed a monastery in Diolcos, Egypt, near the mouth of the Nile River. Piamun, he said, was "the elder of all the anchorites living there and their priest. He was like a tall lighthouse. For he was set on the top of a high mountain like that city in the gospel, and at once he shed his light on our faces."

But it was not only in Egypt. The symbol of the lighthouse shone as brightly as far away as Rome, and even in the dark of the catacombs.

Ancient Sources:

- *Hermas, **Shepherd**, Visions 3.2, 3.3-5.*
- *St. Basil, **Letter** 82.*
- *St. John Cassian, **Conferences** 3.18.1*

Chapter 21
The Ankh

⌗

Give no thought to your goods,
for the best of all the land of Egypt is yours.
Genesis 45:20

At the time of Christ and throughout the era of the Church Fathers, the dominant culture in Egypt was Greek — or at least "Greekish," that is, Hellenistic. Alexander the Great had conquered the country in 331 B.C. as he and his armies rolled eastward to India. His general Ptolemy took the throne of the pharaohs, and Ptolemy's dynasty ruled Egypt till the suicide of the famous Cleopatra VII in 30 B.C.

Over the course of three centuries, Greek language came to dominate the land, as did Greek literature, architecture, and cuisine. Even the old gods were recast in a Greek mold. Yet some vestiges of the old ways remained, especially among Egypt's ancestral people, the Copts.

"Coptic" means, simply, Egyptian. The Ptolemies may have conquered the pharaohs' throne, but the Copts held fast to pharaonic culture, language, religion — and to ancient symbols, such as the ankh. The ankh was the hieroglyphic character that stood for life. (The Romans called it *crux ansata*, a cross with a loop or handle.) Popular as a piece of jewelry, it was believed to have talismanic power, ensuring long life on earth and a happy afterlife as well. It is ubiquitous in religious sculpture, and it is commonly found among the tombs and even in the hands of mummies.

The New Testament shows that Egypt received the Gospel very early. Some of those who converted were certainly Jews, like Apollos of Alexandria, the eloquent "super-apostle" of the first generation (see Acts 18:24; 1 Cor 3-4; Titus 3:13). The great biblical commentator Philo testifies to a thriving and diverse Jewish population in first-century Alexandria,

Coptic tombstone. Egypt.
The Coptic Museum, Cairo.

Rhodia Orant. Funerary stela with Rhodia as Orant from Kom Bultijeh, Egypt (now in the Staatliche Museen, Berlin). Sixth century.

including a remarkable contemplative community called the Therapeutai. Christians who read his accounts cannot help but see these Jews as kindred spirits. Some Fathers of the Church held that the Therapeutai converted en masse. Some modern scholars believe that the Therapeutai liturgy was the immediate forerunner of the Coptic liturgy.

But conversions likely came from the Greeks as well. There is strong evidence that Christian speculative theology may have taken its first missteps in the city of Alexandria, which was then the intellectual capital of the world. And those first missteps were characteristically Greek, an uncontrolled application of Plato's philosophy to Hebrew religion. Still, it takes an energetic religious culture to produce theologians, even wayward ones. Egypt's desert sands have turned up some of the earliest New Testament texts we possess, and they are written in Greek.

The rural lands beside the Nile also proved fertile ground for Christianity. And it is possible that the people who responded in greatest numbers were Egypt's aboriginal people — now second-class citizens in their ancestral lands. Early on, Coptic Christianity showed the signs that have enabled its survival through millennia of persecution. The faith of the Copts was (as it remains today) tenacious, intense, liturgical, and contemplative. Their lands yielded the Church's first famous hermits and its first great monastic communities.

The Copts' conversion ran deep, but they also held fast to many pious customs of their pre-Christian ancestors. There is evidence that early Egyptian Christians continued the practice of embalming their dead. They often painted portraits of the dead upon the burial shrouds and the walls of the tombs. Sometimes the dead are depicted holding the ankh, now understood to be a symbol of the resurrection and of heaven. The symbol appears frequently in Coptic art and crafts, such as lamps and rings. The ankh has even turned up among the graffiti in the ancient tombs of Rome — scrawled, no doubt, as the distinctive mark of Christian pilgrims from faraway Egypt. It was a useful and almost universal symbol, because it also resembled the merging of the Greek letters *tau* (T) and *rho* (P), which together stood as a symbol of victory — especially in the tropaeum, or "trophy" standard carried by a victorious army.

Around the middle of the third century, the Egyptian people ceased using hieroglyphics in their inscriptions. Nevertheless, they continued

Ankh crosses. Coptic textile. Egypt.

inscribing the ankh, and this was increasingly true as the Copts converted to Christianity.

Quite recently, archeologists discovered the mummified remains of a young boy, who was entombed with the complete Book of Psalms as his pillow. Inside the book was an ankh-shaped piece of ivory, which served the dual purpose of a book marker and a consolation to the bereaved: a symbol of life after death.

In the hands of the river god Hapi, the ankh had been considered the "key of the Nile." In Egyptian mythology, it was the key-shaped ankh that unlocked the river's floodgates every year and made the valleys fertile.

To the early Christians of Egypt, the ankh surely suggested the cross of Christ — the historical key to the baptismal waters that were only just beginning to flood the world (see Jn 19:34).

The river god Hapi holding ankh crosses. Egypt.

Magical diptychon. Lead. Museo Ostiense, Ostia, Italy.

The ankh still appears often in Coptic Christian art and church decoration. The symbol's association with Christianity, it seems, has given it new life.

"This was to fulfill what the Lord had spoken by the prophet, 'Out of Egypt have I called my son'" (Mt 2:15).

Ancient Sources:

- Philo of Alexandria, *The Contemplative Life.*
- Sozomen, **Church History** *1.12-13, 3.14.*

Modern Sources:

- *Pearson and Goehring, 39.*
- *Frend, 110.*
- *Frankfurter, 1-3.*
- *Mazza,* **Celebration** *41-44.*

Chapter 22
The Cross

☙

For the word of the cross is folly to those who are perishing,
but to us who are being saved it is the power of God.
1 Corinthians 1:18

There are two schools of thought concerning the use of the cross as a visual symbol in the early Church. One school sees it almost everywhere. The other sees it almost nowhere.

Why this great divergence, when both groups of scholars are dealing with the same small body of evidence?

The primary reason is that simple, clear, and indisputable images of the cross appear very rarely in Christian settings, especially compared with other symbols, such as the orant and the fish. The scarcity is even more striking when we compare the artistic remains of the first four centuries with the Christian culture of the subsequent millennium and a half, when the cross reigned as the dominant symbol of Christianity.

There is a lively dispute about the actual number of crosses in the archeological record. Since some of the proposed items are graffiti, they are hastily scrawled or scratched onto walls — lopsided, rough, old, rugged crosses.

Or perhaps they are not crosses at all. What appear to wishful eyes as the memorial of redemption could be the merely ornamental intersection of perpendicular lines, a common enough pattern in decoration. Or they could be random scuff marks from down the centuries.

In some Christian graffiti, pilgrims seem to have given special emphasis to the letter T and X, embellishing them to resemble a cross. Or maybe not.

The earliest scene of Calvary.
Stone graffito. Iruña-Veleia, Basque country, Spain. Third century.

Supposed imprint of a cross on a wall.
The Casa del Bicentenario, Herculaneum, Italy. Before A.D. 79.

Cross pendant.
Bronz. Tomb in Galilee, Israel. Sixth century.

In the frescoes of the catacombs, loaves of bread seem to be marked with a cross. But can we be sure?

In 1938 archeologists unearthed a house that had been buried deep in lava from the volcanic eruption of Mount Vesuvius in A.D. 79. The wall of a second-story room bore a clear, dark imprint of a cross. In front of the marking were the charred remains of a piece of wooden furniture, which some say was once an altar or a kneeler. Yet others believe that the imprint came from nothing more than a common metal wall bracket — not a sacred object, but a piece of hardware.

The earliest clear visual representation of the cross survives, oddly enough, in a vile piece of anti-Christian graffiti on Palatine Hill in Rome. It crudely portrays a donkey hanging on a cross, over the caption "Alexamenos worships his god." Indeed, the worship of a crucified donkey was among the wild rumors that circulated about the secret rites of Christians. Tertullian mentions this canard once, in order to dismiss it out of hand.

But the charge of secrecy had some basis in fact, and that may help to explain the scarcity of images.

The Church did forbid its members to discuss certain rites and doctrines publicly. Modern historians call this the "discipline of the secret." We find the phenomenon frequently in ancient homilies, when the author

Doorknob attached to a cross.
Bronze. Western Wall excavations, Jerusalem. Byzantine period.

will suddenly break off a discussion with the acknowledgment that there are unbaptized people in the congregation. The Egyptian theologian Origen interrupts a discussion of the Eucharist with the line: "He who is inspired by the mysteries knows both the flesh and the blood of the Word of God. Therefore, let us not remain in these matters, which are known to the wise and cannot be laid open to the ignorant."

The discipline applied mostly to the doctrines that could be easily misunderstood or used in some twisted way against the Christians. The doctrine of the real presence, for example, fed pagan rumors that the Christians were cannibals, eating a man's flesh and drinking his blood.

It is possible that the discipline applied also to the cross, which has always been folly and a stumbling block to unbelievers. It is clear from the works of the early Christian apologists that the cross was an object of derision for the pagans. The Roman rabble taunted Christians for worshiping an executed criminal.

For there was no more grotesque way to be executed. The ancient Romans had a special genius for torture, and crucifixion was the utmost refinement of their art. The Jewish historian Josephus called it "the most wretched of deaths." It was designed to cause the most pain in the most parts of the body over the longest period of time. The cross was humiliating, too, so it was usually reserved for slaves, noncitizens, lower-class criminals, or those whose crimes were especially heinous. The stripped man was exposed, naked, to a boorish crowd that delighted in such spectacles. They cast stones at him, spat at him, jeered at him.

The victim found himself suspended above the ground, his body slumped forward, his knees bent and his feet positioned as if he were standing on tiptoe. That position made it almost impossible for him to draw a breath. He could not inhale or exhale without using the nails in his wrists to pull his body upward, simultaneously pushing up from the nail in his feet. With every breath, he felt the coarse metal tearing at his nerves.

Gradually, his limbs cramped and weakened. As he was less able to lift himself, he began, slowly, to suffocate.

Thus, a victim of crucifixion alternated between the panicked sense of asphyxiation and the searing pain of the nails in his flesh. Relief from one inevitably brought about the agony of the other. In a strong man, this could go on for many hours, even days.

Executions took place in public venues. So crucifixion would have

Funerary stela. Monastery of St. Jeremias, Egypt
(now in the Coptic Museum, Cairo). Third – fourth century.

Fragment of a lead coffin.
Israel Antiquities Authority. Fourth century.

been a familiar sight to many of the early Christians. This, too, may account for the dearth of crosses in the archeological record. Those who had seen a man crucified would hardly need to gaze at a reminder when they attended Sunday Mass. They already knew the price of their redemption.

Only when we know the horror of the cross can we recognize the shock value of of St. Paul's claim to "glory . . . in the cross of our Lord Jesus Christ" (Gal 6:14).

An excavation in the Spain's Basque region recently turned up an extremely rare pre-Constantinian depiction of the ordeal of the cross. The earliest devotional cross of which we are certain, the Iruña Veleia inscription is a primitive, but detailed panorama of the hilltop scene at Calvary. It depicts Jesus crucified between two others, while two more figures (Mary and John) stand at the foot of the cross. It was almost certainly carved in the third century.

Yet the Iruña Veleia image is an anomaly, so far unique in the archeological record. The only images comparable are the "staurograms," or cross-monograms, interspersed in some New Testament manuscripts.

When abbreviating the Greek words for "cross" and "crucify" (*stauros* and *stauroo*), Christian scribes would sometimes combine the letters *tau* and *rho*, so that together they resembled a man on a gibbet. The scholar Larry Hurtado argues, very persuasively, that these are the oldest Christian "images" we possess today.

Nevertheless, we can be sure that, from the first generation onward, the cross stood firm at the center of Christian spirituality. Around A.D. 100, St. Ignatius of Antioch wrote: "As for me, my spirit is now all humble devotion to the cross — the cross which so greatly offends the unbelievers, but is salvation and eternal life to us."

If the symbol was absent from their walls, it was never far from the Christians' lips, hearts, and minds. Many of the Fathers testify to the custom of tracing the sign of the cross on one's forehead. Tertullian exhorted his readers to begin and end all their humdrum activities by tracing the holy sign: "At every step forward and movement, at every going in and going out, when we put on our clothes and shoes, when we bathe, when we sit at table, when we light the lamps, on couch, on seat, in all the ordinary actions of daily life, we trace upon the forehead the sign."

Elsewhere, he taught that the cross was the sign foretold by the

Part of a mosaic floor depicting a cross and fish.
Church at Shavei Ziyyon, Israel. Fifth century.

Palatine cross — "Alexamenos worships his god." Anti-Christian graffito
from the Palatine Hill, Rome. Museo delle Terme. End of the second century.

Prophet Ezekiel: "Pass through the city and mark a tau on the foreheads of those who moan and groan over all the abominations that are practiced within" (Ezk 9:3-4). The Book of Revelation, in turn, speaks of Christians as those who have "the seal of God upon their foreheads" (Rev 9:4). Tertullian wrote: "Now the Greek letter tau and our own letter T is the very form of the cross, which [God] predicted would be the sign on our foreheads in the true Catholic Jerusalem."

Tertullian's contemporary, St. Clement of Alexandria, also spoke of the cross as the pre-eminent "symbol of the Lord."

Why, then, does it appear so seldom on the walls and lamps, the cups and documents of the early Christians?

The Fathers themselves suggest another hypothesis. Perhaps the cross is everywhere, and it is hidden in plain sight. It is in the images that some scholars call "crypto-crosses" — crosses disguised as elements of more benign and ordinary objects. The more philosophically inclined of the Fathers held that the cross could be discerned everywhere, because the very fabric of the cosmos was inscribed with the cross. As proof of this, they often cited Plato's account of the creation of the universe, fashioned, he believed, by a divine being called the Demiurge. The Demiurge conceived all reality as turning on horizontal and vertical axes: "He split all this that He had put together into two parts lengthwise; and then He laid the twain one against the other, the middle of one to the middle of the other, like a great cross." The Fathers believed this passage from the *Timaeus* to be Plato's "prophecy of the cross" of Jesus Christ. Commenting on this ancient interpretation, Cardinal Joseph Ratzinger said: "The Cross of Golgotha is foreshadowed in the structure of the universe itself. The instrument of torment on which the Lord died is written into the structure of the universe. The cosmos speaks to us of the Cross, and the Cross solves for us the enigma of the cosmos. It is the real key to all reality."

And so it was. "Think for a moment," said St. Justin, around A.D. 155, "and ask yourself if the business of the world could be carried on without the figure of the cross. The sea cannot be crossed unless this sign of

Marble reliquary with a sliding lid, decorated with crosses.
Eastern Mediterranean. Fifth–seventh century.

victory — the mast — be unharmed. Without it there is no plowing; neither diggers nor mechanics can do their work without tools of this shape; . . . The power of this form is shown by your own symbols, on your banners and trophies, which are the insignia of your power and government."

A few years later, Minucius Felix sketched the same listing of places where Christians "assuredly see the sign of the cross in nature" and even in pagan religion! "Thus," he concluded, "the sign of the cross either is sustained by a natural reason, or your own religion is formed with respect to it."

The problem with crypto-crosses is that we can never know for sure what the original artist intended. Did he want us to see a cross — or just an anchor? That uncertainty, however, applies to many other ancient symbols as well, and leaves us with the question of whether we can know anything at all.

Crypto-crosses may be difficult to defend before the academic community, but before God we cannot go too far wrong by looking for the cross of Christ everywhere in life — not least in the catacombs that were built by the martyrs to hold the bones of the martyrs.

———

Ancient Sources:
- *Plato,* **Timaeus** *36b.*
- *Origen,* **On Leviticus** *10.*
- *Josephus,* **Jewish Wars** *7.203.*
- *St. Ignatius of Antioch,* **Ephesians** *18.1.*
- *Tertullian,* **The Chaplet** *3.3;* **Against Marcion** *3.22.*
- *St. Clement of Alexandria,* **Tapestries** *6.*
- *St. Justin Martyr,* **First Apology** *55.*
- *Minucius Felix,* **Octavius** *29.*

Modern Sources:
- *Hurtado, 135-154.*
- *Jensen,* **Understanding** *133-141.*
- *Ratzinger, 181.*
- *Snyder, 58-64.*

Ladle-strainer with a cross.

Silver and enamel (University of Toronto, Malcove Collection). Fifth–sixth century.

Chapter 23
The Anchor

☙

We have this as a sure and steadfast anchor of the soul,
a hope that enters into the inner shrine behind the curtain,
where Jesus has gone as a forerunner on our behalf,
having become a high priest forever.
Hebrews 6:19-20

As the Jews were not a seafaring people, we do not encounter much nautical imagery in the Hebrew Scriptures. The word "anchor" does not appear in the Bible until the New Testament, whose characters include so many fishermen and world travelers. Anchors serve as key props in the story of the storm at sea told in chapter 27 of the Acts of the Apostles. The only overtly metaphorical mention of an anchor is in the Hebrews passage quoted above, where the anchor stands for hope of salvation and everlasting life.

This hope seems to be the primary symbolic meaning of the anchors that appear everywhere in early Christian funerary art. The anchor represents the state of a soul that has reached its destination in tranquil waters — that has reached peace in the port of eternity. The anchor represents stability after a lifetime of uncertainty and change. Yet it also represents peace in this life, as the Christian is already living within sight of the port.

St. Augustine developed the image rather poetically: "We are already there in our longing. We throw our hope, like an anchor, into that land before us, lest we suffer shipwreck in this sea where we are tossed about. We rightly say, as we would of a ship at anchor, that she has come to land. She still rolls, but she has been brought safe to land in the teeth of winds and storms. So, against the temptations of this sojourning, our

Anchor and two fish.
Marble titulus from the Catacombs of Priscilla, Rome. Second–third century.

Anchor with alpha and omega.
Graffito from the Catacombs of Domitilla, Rome.

hope is grounded in that city Jerusalem and keeps us from being carried away upon the rocks."

As Christianity spread through the Mediterranean, its preachers and teachers more frequently drew metaphors from seafaring life. Thus, in the work of St. Hippolytus of Rome, the anchor appears as part of an extended nautical allegory, and it symbolizes the stabilizing power of the commandments, "which are strong as iron."

St. Clement of Alexandria recognizes the anchor as a suitable emblem for Christian seals and signets, even though he acknowledges it as the heraldry of the pagan Macedonian general Seleucus.

The anchor symbolizes hope of salvation; but Christians almost always drew, carved, or painted their anchors in a cruciform shape. For the cross was their hope of salvation. It is likely that many, if not all, of the Christian anchors are crypto-crosses. When we see the figure of a dolphin

Hesperos inscription.
The Catacombs of St. Callistus — Crypts of Lucina, Rome. Beginning of third century.

(a common symbol of Jesus Christ) wrapped around an anchor, we are gazing on a deeply symbolic crypto-crucifix.

Ancient Sources:

- St. Augustine, **On the Psalms** 65.3.
- St. Hippolytus, **Antichrist** 59.
- St. Clement, **The Teacher** 3.11.59.

Epitaph of Faustinianus.
The Catacombs of St. Callistus — Crypts of Lucina, Rome. Second–third century.

Chapter 24
Ships and Boats

☙

The waters prevailed and increased greatly upon the earth;
and the ark floated on the face of the waters.
Genesis 7:18

The ship (or boat) is among the few symbols that St. Clement of Alexandria approved for the seals and signets of Christians. It symbolized the Church, and there are strong scriptural reasons for the association. Even today, Catholics refer to the Church as the "barque of Peter," evoking the fishing boats the apostle sails in the Gospels (Mk 6:45, e.g., and Jn 21:3).

Early Christian art often portrays the ship of the Church as Noah's ark, and this image surely draws from the First Epistle of Peter, which offers Noah's story as a foreshadowing of baptism, which is the duty of the Church. In baptism, as in the ark, people are "saved through water" (1 Pet 3:20-21). The Letter to the Hebrews also discusses the ark in "saving" terms (Heb 11:7).

The early Christians could not conceive of salvation apart from the sacraments, and they could not conceive of the sacraments apart from the Church. These notions all converged in the image of the ship — the wooden vessel that brought people safely through water.

For St. Justin Martyr, the matter came down to three elements: water, faith, and wood. "For Christ," said St. Justin Martyr, "became the chief of another race regenerated by Himself through water, faith, and wood, containing the mystery of the cross. Just as when Noah was saved by wood he rode over the waters with his household." Elsewhere, Justin explains that the "mystery of the cross" — the hidden cross — is the cru-

Noah.
Fragment of a sarcophagus found near St. Sebastian, Rome. The Vatican Museum.

ciform shape of every ship's mast. With these crypto-crosses borne aloft, even the pagan vessels glorified Jesus Christ.

For Tertullian, the ship of the Church harks back to the tempest-tossed boat on the Sea of Galilee, where Jesus calmed the storm (Mk 6:45ff). "That little ship," he said, "presented a figure of the Church, which is disquieted 'in the sea,' that is, in the world, 'by the waves,' that is, by persecutions and temptations. The Lord patiently sleeps, as it were, till roused by the prayers of the saints, who have reached their limit. He checks the world and restores tranquillity to His own."

In another place, Tertullian took up the image of Noah's ark and developed it as a rather extensive allegory. Like the ark, the Church can accommodate a wide diversity of peoples — and these people must clamber onto the ark if they wish to be saved. But, warned Tertullian, they must leave their idols behind. There must be no place for idolatry in the Church.

> Amid reefs and inlets, amid shallows and straits of idolatry, faith navigates. Her sails are filled by the Spirit of God. She is safe if cautious, secure if intently watchful. But those who are washed overboard fall into a deep from which there is no escape. Those who are run aground are inextricably shipwrecked. Those

Small boat.
Graffito from the Catacombs of St. Callistus, Rome. Third century.

Jonah and Noah. Detail from the Sarcophagus of Junia Julia Juliane(te?)
dedicated by her husband. The Vatican Museum. Before A.D. 313.

who are engulfed find themselves in a whirlpool where
there can be no breathing . . . All waves suffocate them.
Every eddy sucks them down to hell . . . No idolater is
found in the original type of the ark: no animal has
been fashioned to represent an idol. Let nothing be in
the Church that was not in the Ark.

Hippolytus of Rome also developed the figure of the ship into an
elaborate allegory. He concentrated not on the dangers in the water, as
Tertullian had, but rather on the parts and personnel of the ship, finding
correspondences everywhere in the Church. "The sea," he said, "is the world
in which the Church is set, like a ship tossed in the deep, but not destroyed;
for she has with her the skilled Pilot, Christ." Like Justin, he described the
cruciform mast. He pointed to the "prow" facing east, like the altars of
the ancient churches. The Church's "tillers" are the two testaments of the
Bible. The ropes are the love of Christ, which binds Christians. The net
is the baptismal font, and the wind that fills the sails is the Holy Spirit.
The anchors are the commandments; the sailors, the holy angels; and the
topsails are the prophets, martyrs, and apostles in heaven.

An ancient liturgical manual, the **Apostolic Constitutions**, employs the metaphor as it urges bishops to keep their churches — and even their church buildings — in ship shape: "When you call an assembly of the Church, do so as commander of a great ship . . . Assign the deacons as mariners to prepare places for the congregation with all due care and decency, just as they would for passengers. And let the building be long, with its head to the east, with its vestries on both sides at the east end, and so it will be like a ship. In the middle let the bishop's throne be placed, and on each side of him let the priests sit down; and let the deacons stand nearby . . . for they are like the mariners and managers of the ship."

Some interpreters also see, in Christian ship paintings, a visual echo of pre-Christian pagan images of the boat that ferries the dead to the afterlife.

Ships and boats were, for the Fathers, rich images of the Church — a ship that itself looked back to the ark of Noah, and ahead to dock in heaven.

Jonah. Detail from the Jonah Sarcophagus.
Museo Lateranense, Rome. Late third–early fourth century.

Jesus and apostles in a boat.
Sarcophagus fragment. The Vatican Museum. Fourth century.

Ancient Sources:

- St. Clement of Alexandria, **Christ the Teacher** 3.2.
- St. Justin Martyr, **Dialogue** 138; **First Apology** 55.
- St. Hippolytus, **On Christ and Antichrist** 59.
- Tertullian, **On Baptism** 12.7; **On Idolatry** 24.
- **Apostolic Constitutions** 2.57.

Modern Source:

- Daniélou, **Primitive** 58-70.

Chapter 25
The Labarum (Chi-Rho)

☙

*He who conquers, I will make him a pillar in the temple of
my God . . . and I will write on him the name of my God.*
Revelation 3:12

Labarum is the Latin name commonly applied to the symbol that
combines two Greek letters: X (*chi*) and P (*rho*). These are the first two
letters in the word *christos* (anointed), from which we derive the English
word "Christ."

The word, however, is much older than the Christian symbol it has
come to denote. In pagan antiquity, the Roman armies used the word
labarum to describe any official military standard — the heraldry that
was borne aloft whenever the army assembled. During battle, the legions
fiercely defended these standards, usually assigning the task to the best
trained soldiers. The *labarum* represented the honor, the ideals, and the
basic identity (national and religious) of the legion. And so it usually
depicted symbols of the emperor, his family, and the gods he invoked for
protection.

Such was the standard of Constantine as he entered the decisive
battle of his career. His soldiers had declared him emperor of the west, but
he faced fierce opposition from another general, Maxentius, whose armies
had acclaimed him for the same office. The two men and their armies
battled out the dispute through Europe and North Africa, converging at
Rome in October of A.D. 312. Their final encounter is known as the battle
of the Milvian Bridge, a pontoon bridge that stretches across the Tiber
River.

Maxentius' troops had many advantages — far greater numbers
and a more secure position. Constantine, however, soon outmaneuvered

St. Januarius. The Catacomb of San Gennaro, Naples, Italy. Fifth century.

his opponent; and Maxentius and many of his troops perished when the bridge they were crossing collapsed beneath them. Constantine marched into Rome unopposed — and he himself would later recall that he did so under the labarum of Christ, the chi-rho.

How did Constantine prevail? A scholar of his court, Lactantius, explained that the victory came after Constantine received a vision. "Constantine," he said, "was directed in a dream to cause the heavenly sign to be delineated on the shields of his soldiers, and so to proceed to battle. He did as he had been commanded, and he marked on their shields the letter X, with a perpendicular line drawn through it and turned round at the top, being the cipher of Christ."

A few years later, Eusebius, the historian-bishop of Caesarea, tells a fuller version of the story. According to Eusebius, Constantine was wide awake when he had the initial vision, which came only after the emperor, then a pagan, had directed his most earnest prayer to the God of the Christians. Then, looking into the setting sun, Constantine "saw with his own eyes the trophy of a cross of light in the heavens, above the sun, and bearing the inscription, 'Conquer by this.'" It was not a private revelation, but a public proclamation. Eusebius adds that all of Constantine's troops witnessed the phenomenon as well. Eusebius cites Constantine himself as

VITORA IN PACE — Victoria in peace.
Epitaph from the Roman catacombs. After A.D. 313.

his source, and adds that the emperor had sealed his testimony with an oath.

Constantine testified that Christ then appeared to him — in a dream on the same night — to interpret the omen. The Lord "commanded him to make a likeness of the sign he had seen in the heavens, and to use it as a safeguard in all engagements with his enemies." And in the morning he did. The legion's craftsmen fashioned a new standard out of gold and jewels, and had it ready in time for the day's battle.

"Now it was made in the following manner. A long spear, overlaid with gold, formed the figure of the cross by means of a transverse bar laid over it. On the top of the whole was fixed a wreath of gold and precious stones; and within this, the symbol of the Savior's name, two letters indicating the name of Christ by means of its initial characters, the letter P being intersected by X in its center."

There is some controversy over whether the chi-rho had already been established as a Christian symbol when Constantine adopted it as his own. It does appear, for example, as an abbreviation for "Christ" in manuscripts from the second and third centuries; but we don't know how common or widespread that practice was. The scholar Andre Grabar argued that Constantine was reaching back to "the first Christian attempt

Bowl with labarum.
Terracotta. The Roman catacombs. Around A.D. 350.

Mosaic portrait of Christ. Roman villa at Hinton St. Mary, Dorset England (now in the British museum). Late fourth century.

to create religious figurations . . . symbolic signs . . . image-signs." Larry Hurtado calles them "the earliest Christian iconography."

The symbol also had some secular uses. Scribes used it to mark especially good passages in the books of their favorite authors, as we might use an asterisk today. It might have been an abbreviation for the word *chrestos*, meaning "useful." That's an interesting coincidence, but a common scribal notation is hardly the kind of symbol that would inspire valor in seasoned military veterans. One thing is certain: in the years immediately following Constantine's reported vision, word spread rapidly. In Christian graffiti of the period, the symbol is suddenly commonplace. In the crypt beneath St. Peter's Basilica alone, there are many surviving examples.

Some historians think that Constantine was capitalizing upon the familiar sign of victory, the *tropaeum* (in Greek, *tropaion*), which often depicted an intersecting T (*tau*) and P (*rho*). Many of these conversations turn on whether one believes Constantine was God's providential vindicator — or just a savvy schemer, who saw the Church as a potential unifier and stabilizer for a rapidly crumbling empire. There are conscientious Christians on both sides of the discussion, and even some who take both sides simultaneously, knowing that providence does not operate on the merit system; and Scripture testifies that God often called great sinners to be His prophets and kings.

Coin of Magnentius.
Amiens, France. A.D. 350–353.

In any event, the new *labarum* soon went the way of its predecessors. It appeared on coins and medallions, on military uniforms, and on the walls of civic buildings. Through the generations of Constantine's dynasty, it remained the standard. And it has prevailed, even to our own day, as *the labarum* — the only one we mean when we use the term today — because it became the symbol of Christ's victory over persecutors and their empires, and all their works and all their pomps.

Ancient Sources:
- *Lactantius, **On the Deaths of the Persecutors** 44.*
- *Eusebius, **Life of Constantine** 1.28-31.*

Modern Sources:
- *Guarducci, 75.*
- *Hurtado, 135-152.*
- *Grabar, 38-39.*
- *Walsh, 95-99.*

Ss. Peter and Paul. Epitaph of Asellus from the Catacombs of St. Hippolytus, Rome. Late fourth century. The Vatican Museum.

Loculus graffito from the Catacombs of St. Agnes, Rome.

Chapter 26
Alpha and Omega

⌁

*"I am the Alpha and the Omega," says the Lord God, who is
and who was and who is to come, the Almighty . . . I am the
Alpha and the Omega, the first and the last, the beginning
and the end.*
Revelation 1:8, 22:13

"Everything from A to Z" — It is a commonplace figure of speech,
and it appears almost everywhere there is a written language. When
people want to express completeness and totality, they invoke the first
and last letters of their alphabet. In Greek, those letters are A (*alpha*) and
Ω (*omega*).

Christians have always found such fullness in God alone. In the
Book of Revelation, the last book of the Bible, God three times describes
Himself as the "alpha and omega" (Rev 1:8, 21:6, 22:13). He is "the first and
the last, the beginning and the end" (22:13).

The earliest Christians invoked these lines often because they sum-
marize so much that is distinctive about their God. Unlike the idols of
the pagans, the Christian God is eternal. He transcends time and history.
All time is ever-present to Him. As creator, He is Himself the origin of
all things. As judge and king, He is their goal and their end. Greek and
Roman mythology, on the other hand, described their Olympian gods as
immortal, but not eternal. Their gods had generations and genealogies, as
they took their origin from other gods. Athena, for example, sprang fully
grown from the head of the supreme god Zeus. Apollo was the son of
Zeus and the titan Leto.

Not so the God of Israel. In calling Himself "alpha and omega,"
He speaks in a way that is consistent with His other great moments of

Bust of Christ.
Fresco from the Catacomb of Commodilla, Rome. Mid-to-late fourth century.

Bread stamp.
Stone. Collection of the Wolff Family, Jerusalem, Israel.

self-disclosure. First, He uses a characteristic "I am" statement. In Exodus, God identified Himself to Moses as "I am who am." Thus, God's name denotes the only being that is eternally present. Jesus often echoes this divine name when He speaks of Himself. In John's Gospel, Jesus expresses His divinity and His eternity with "I am" statements: for example, "Before Abraham was, I am" (Jn 8:58; see also 4:26, 8:24, 8:28). Most commentators note that "the first and the last" echoes the words God spoke through Isaiah: "I am the first and I am the last; besides Me there is no god" (Is 44:6; see also 41:4 and 48:12).

Since at least one of the passages in Revelation is spoken by Jesus Himself, the Church Fathers presented this as a testimony to the Savior's divinity and His eternity. St. Clement does so in Alexandria, Egypt, at the end of the second century, as does Tertullian in North Africa. In the next generation, St. Cyprian of Carthage follows. Origen, the Egyptian, cites the passages of Revelation to demonstrate that Jesus is coeternal and coequal with the Father: "So that you may understand that the omnipotence of Father and Son is one and the same, as God and the Lord are one and the same with the Father, listen to the manner in which John speaks in Revelation."

The Book of Revelation offered great hope to Christians living in troubled times. In it God — who is eternal, all-powerful, and all-knowing — guaranteed the victory of the faithful over their persecutors.

Triple labarum and triple alpha and omega. Mosaic in the baptistery of Albenga in Liguria, Italy. End of the fifth–beginning of the sixth century.

Thus the alpha-omega symbol was a source of courage, a reminder of the Christian's hidden reservoir of strength.

The letters appear commonly as decorations in ancient places of worship and especially at burial sites. Some alpha-omega graffiti may date all the way back to the first century. In later examples, the letters often flank the chi-rho, thus symbolizing the victory of Christ as the climax of human history. Sometimes, each of the letters is repeated three times, thus representing the coeternal Trinity of divine persons. The alpha and omega appear also with other symbols, such as the wreath, the lamb, or the name of Jesus Christ. The symbol grew enormously popular in the early fourth century, as a visual refutation of the heretical doctrine of Arius, the Alexandrian priest who denied the full divinity and co-eternity of

God the Son. In the centuries that followed, the letters appeared together everywhere — in church decoration, on signet rings, on liturgical vessels, and especially on coins.

These letters represent the wellsprings of Christian hope. Because Christ is divine and eternal, He alone can conquer the inevitable and otherwise invincible enemy, which is death.

In Rome there are several curious examples of these two Greek letters. They appear at gravesites — not in the usual order, but reversed: as omega-alpha. Archeologists believe that the reversal is itself symbolic, and profoundly meaningful in its context. Mourners scratched them into plaster at the tombs of the martyrs. They did so because they knew that Christ alone could bring a new beginning from the cruel finality of death. Those who died in Christ would surely know a new beginning in Him. St. Clement of Alexandria said that Jesus is "the Alpha and the Omega of whom alone the end becomes beginning, and ends again at the original beginning without any break."

Origen wrote that early visionaries glimpsed the meaning of the letters written in heaven. God's letters, he said, "which the saints read and say they have read what is written in the tablets of heaven, those letters are the thoughts about the Son of God which are broken up into alpha

Fragment of a lintel from a church doorway.
Limestone. Syria. A.D. 400–550.

Stela with omega and alpha.
Stone. Arles, Les Alyscamps, France. After A.D. 313.

and the letters that follow to omega, that heavenly matters might be read through them."

Thus, he held that alpha-omega serves as an abbreviation and an anticipation. It is shorthand for the beginning, the end, and everything in between — the fullness of time and of creation. And it looks to the day when Christ will be "all in all" (1 Cor 15:28), the day that is here already in eternity, but not yet in time, here in faith, but not yet in vision.

Ancient Sources:

Tertullian, **On Monogamy** 5; **Against Praxeas** 17.

Clement, **Tapestries** 4.25, 6.16.

Cyprian, **Testimonies** 2.1, 2.4.

Origen, **First Principles** 1.2.10.

Modern Sources:

Walsh, 97.

Lampe, 9.

Works Consulted

⚜

Allison, Dale. *The New Moses*. Minneapolis, MN: Fortress, 1993.

Apostolos-Cappadona, Diane. *Dictionary of Christian Art*. New York: Continuum, 1994.

Aquilina, Mike. *The Fathers of the Church: An Introduction to the First Christian Teachers*. Huntington, IN: Our Sunday Visitor, 1999.

Aquilina, Mike. *The Mass of the Early Christians*. Huntington, IN: Our Sunday Visitor, 2002.

Aquilina, Mike. *The Resilient Church*. Ijamsville, MD: Word Among Us, 2007.

Aquilina, Mike. *The Way of the Fathers: Praying with the Early Christians*. Huntington, IN: Our Sunday Visitor, 2000.

Aringhi, Paolo. *Roma Subterranea Novissima*. Oregon: Collegium Graphicum, 1972.

Baruffa, Antonio. *The Catacombs of St. Callistus*. Vatican: Libreria Editrice Vaticana, 2000.

Bisconti, Fabrizio, editor. *Temi di Iconografia Paleocristiana*. Citta del Vaticano: PIAC, 2000.

Bradshaw, Paul F. *Eucharistic Origins*. Oxford: Oxford University, 2004.

Brettman, Estelle Shohet. *Vaults of Memory: Jewish and Christian Imagery in the Catacombs of Rome*. Boston: International Catacomb Society, 1985.

Brightman, F.E., *Liturgies Eastern and Western*. Oxford: Clarendon Press, 1896.

Charbonneau-Lassay, Louis. *The Bestiary of Christ*. New York: Parabola, 1991.

Cuming, Geoffrey J., editor. *The Liturgy of St. Mark*. Rome: Pontifical Oriental Institute, 1990.

Daniélou, Jean. *The Bible and the Liturgy*. Notre Dame, IN: University of Notre Dame Press, 1956.

Daniélou, Jean. *Primitive Christian Symbols*. Baltimore: Helicon, 1961.

Daniélou, Jean. *The Theology of Jewish Christianity*. Chicago: Regnery, 1964.

Donfried, Karl P., and Peter Richardson, editors. *Judaism and Christianity in First-Century Rome*. Grand Rapids, MI: Eerdmans, 1998.

Downey, Glanville. *Ancient Antioch*. Princeton, NJ: Princeton University Press, 1963.

Du Bourguet, Pierre. *The Art of the Copts*. New York: Crown, 1967.

Du Bourguet, Pierre. *Coptic Art*. London: Methuen, 1971.

Engelbrecht, Edward. "God's Milk: An Orthodox Confession of the Eucharist." *Journal of Early Christian Studies* 7.4 (1999), 509-526.

Ferguson, George. *Signs and Symbols in Christian Art*. London: Oxford, 1961.

Finaldi, Gabriele. *The Image of Christ*. London: National Gallery, 2000.

Finegan, Jack. *Light from the Ancient Past: The Archeological Background of the Hebrew-Christian Religion*. London: Oxford, 1954.

Frankfurter, David. *Elijah in Upper Egypt*. Minneapolis, MN: Fortress, 1993.

Frend, W.H.C. *The Early Church*. Minneapolis, MN: Fortress, 1982.

Gabra, Gawdat, and Marianne Eaton-Krauss. *The Treasures of Coptic Art in the Coptic Museum and Churches of Old Cairo*. Cairo: American University in Cairo Press, 2007.

Ginzberg, Louis. *Legends of the Bible*. Philadelphia: Jewish Publication Society, 1992.

Goodenough, Erwin. *Jewish Symbols in the Greco-Roman Period*. Volumes 5-6: Fish, Bread, and Wine. New York: Pantheon Books, 1956.

Goodenough, Erwin [edited and abridged by Jacob Neusner]. *Jewish Symbols in the Greco-Roman Period*. Princeton, NJ: Princeton University, 1988.

Grabar, André. *Christian Iconography: A Study of Its Origins*. Princeton, NJ: Princeton University Press, 1968.

Griggs. C. Wilfred. *Early Egyptian Christianity: From Its Origins to 451 C.E.* Leiden: Brill, 1988.

Guarducci, Margherita. *The Primacy of the Church of Rome: Documents, Reflections, Proofs.* San Francisco: Ignatius, 2003.

Hahn, Scott. "Kingdom and Church in Luke-Acts: From Davidic Christology to Kingdom Ecclesiology," in *Reading Luke: Interpretation, Reflection, Formation.* Edited by Craig G. Bartholomew et al. Grand Rapids, MI: Zondervan, 2005, 294-326.

Hahn, Scott. *The Lamb's Supper.* New York: Doubleday, 1999.

Hahn, Scott, and Mike Aquilina. *Living the Mysteries.* Huntington, IN: Our Sunday Visitor, 2003.

Haig, Elizabeth. *The Floral Symbolism of the Great Masters.* London: Kegan Paul, Trench Trubner, 1913.

Hertling, Ludwig, and Engelbert Kirschbaum. *The Roman Catacombs and Their Martyrs.* Milwaukee: Bruce, 1956.

Hurtado, Larry W. *The Earliest Christian Artifacts: Manuscripts and Christian Origins.* Grand Rapids, MI: Eerdmans, 2006.

Israeli, Yael. *Cradle of Christianity.* Jerusalem: The Israel Museum, 2000.

Jensen, Robin Margaret. *Face to Face: Portraits of the Divine in Early Christianity.* Minneapolis: Fortress, 2005.

Jensen, Robin Margaret. *Understanding Early Christian Art.* London: Routledge, 2000.

Jungmann, Joseph. *The Mass of the Roman Rite: Its Origins and Development* (two volumes). New York: Benziger, 1951.

Kaniyamparampil, Emmanuel. *The Spirit of Life: A Study of the Holy Spirit in the Early Syriac Tradition.* Kerala, India: Oriental Institute of Religious Studies India, 2003.

Kondoleon, Christine. *Antioch: The Lost Ancient City.* Princeton: Princeton University Press, 2000.

Lampe, Peter. *From Paul to Valentinus: Christians at Rome in the First Two Centuries.* Minneapolis: Fortress Press, 2003.

Loosley, Emma. "Archaeology and Cultural Belonging in Contemporary

Syria: The Value of Archaeology to Religious Minorities," in *World Archaeology*, Volume 37.4 (December 2005), 589-596.

Mancinelli, Fabrizio. *The Catacombs of Rome and the Origins of Christianity.* Firenze: Scala, 1981.

Marucchi, Orazio. *Manual of Christian Archeology.* Paterson, NJ: St. Anthony Guild, 1949.

Mathews, Thomas F. *The Clash of Gods: A Reinterpretation of Early Christian Art.* Princeton: Princeton University Press, 2003.

Mazza, Enrico. *The Celebration of the Eucharist: The Origin of the Rite and the Development of Its Interpretation.* Collegeville, MN: Pueblo, 1999.

Mazza, Enrico. *The Origins of the Eucharistic Prayer.* Collegeville, MN: Pueblo, 1995.

Milburn, Robert. *Early Christian Art and Architecture.* Berkeley: University of California Press, 1988.

Murphy, Mable Gant. *Nature Allusions in the Works of Clement of Alexandria.* Washington: Catholic University of America, 1941.

Murray, Peter and Linda. *The Oxford Companion to Christian Art and Architecture.* New York: Oxford, 1996.

Murray, Robert. *Symbols of Church and Kingdom: A Study in Early Syriac Tradition.* Piscataway, NJ: Gorgias, 1975.

Musurillo, Herbert. *Symbolism and the Christian Imagination.* Baltimore: Helicon, 1962.

Musurillo, Herbert, translator and editor. *The Acts of the Christian Martyrs.* London: Oxford, 1972.

Neusner, Jacob, editor. *Dictionary of Judaism in the Biblical Period.* Peabody, MA: Hendrickson, 1999.

Pearson, Birger A., and James E. Goehring, editors. *The Roots of Egyptian Christianity.* Philadelphia: Fortress, 1992.

Plumpe, Joseph C. *Mater Ecclesia: An Inquiry into the Concept of the Church as Mother in Early Christianity.* Washington: Catholic University of America, 1943.

Ratzinger, Joseph Cardinal. *The Spirit of the Liturgy.* San Francisco: Ignatius, 2000.

Salonius, A.H., editor. *Martyrium Beati Petri Apostoli a Lino Episcopo Conscripturm.* Helsinki, 1926.

Scaglia, Sisto. *The Catacombs of Saint Callistus: History and Description.* Grottaferrata: Scuola Tipografica Italo-Orientale, 1923.

Simon, Marcel. *Verus Israel: A Study of the Relations Between Christians and Jews in the Roman Empire AD 135-425.* London: Valentine Mitchell, 1996.

Smith, Dennis E. *From Symposium to Eucharist: The Banquet in the Early Christian World.* Minneapolis, MN: Fortress, 2003.

Snyder, Graydon F. *Ante Pacem: Archaeological Evidence of Church Life Before Constantine.* Atlanta: Mercer University, 2005.

van der Meer, F. *Atlas of the Early Christian World.* London: Nelson, 1959.

Visser, Margaret. *The Geometry of Love: Space, Time, Mystery, and Meaning in an Ordinary Church.* New York: North Point, 2000.

Walsh, John E. *The Bones of St. Peter.* Manila: Sinag-Tala, 1987.

Webber, F.R. *Church Symbolism.* Cleveland, OH: J.H. Jansen, 1938.

Weitzmann, Kurt. *Late Antique and Early Christian Book Illumination.* New York: George Braziller, 1977.

Yarnold, Edward. *The Awe-Inspiring Rites of Initiation.* Collegeville, MN: Liturgical Press, 1994.